The Girl That Floats

Annotated

Memories of an Iowa Pioneer Girl

The Girl That Floats

Annotated

Memories of an Iowa Pioneer Girl

By Mary Ann Maulsby Mills

Edited and annotated by Rachelle L. Tuttle

Published by Tallgrass Prairie Books

https://www.tallgrassprairiebooks.com

info@tallgrassprairiebooks.com

ISBN: 979-8-9905605-1-2

Library of Congress Control Number: 202491044511

Notice: The information in this book is true and complete to the best of our knowledge. It is offered without guarantee on the part of the author or Tallgrass Prairie Books. The author and Tallgrass Prairie Books disclaim all liability in connection with the use of this book.

Book design and annotations by Rachelle L. Tuttle.

Cover design by Travis Biggs

Dedication

I dedicate this book to all the pioneers of yesteryear, who, weary and tired, none the less forged their way into lands unknown. They packed all they owned and headed into unfamiliar territory in the hopes of having their own piece of land in which to build homes, farms, ranches and futures. Their stories speak of a life that in this modern day we cannot imagine. Only through journals, diaries and letters can we even begin to envision their lives, so these works are priceless.

"Much has been written of the pioneers of the West, and many words of praise spoken, but too much cannot be said commendatory of the brave men and women who left homes in the East, where they were surrounded by every evidence of civilized life, together with friends and kindred, and came into a new and almost unknown country, redeeming it from the wily red men and preparing it for their children and children's children that should come after them. But little more than a half century ago that portion of Iowa, "the beautiful land," now comprising the wealthy county of Washington, was an unbroken wilderness, in habited by wild beasts, wild fowl and no less wild red men. Its forests had not resounded with the woodman's ax, nor its prairie been uptorn by the plow. All was then as it came from the hand of the Creator."

Portrait and Biographical Album of Washington County, Iowa, Brookhaven Press, 1887

In equal part, I dedicate this book to the resilient and enduring spirit of the Native American peoples of the United States. We must acknowledge the grave injustices inflicted upon them in the name of Manifest Destiny. From forced removal from their native homelands to broken treaties and loss of cultural heritage and traditions, the wounds of the past run deep. Their ancestral lands bore witness to both the beauty and brutality of history.

Rachelle Tuttle, Editor

Table of Contents

Preface

Other than editing for clarity, punctuation, and adding chapter titles, the following writing is presented as originally written. It has been my intent to keep Mary Ann's words her own.

I have been tracing my family roots for nearly three decades. I was incredibly blessed to have been given mountains of material from those who did the work the hard way – by visiting cemeteries, historical societies, court houses and libraries. There was no Internet for them of course, and their work was a great labor of love. I am forever grateful.

When researching the Hollingsworth branch of my family, I became enthralled with the story of their migration to Keokuk County, Iowa circa 1840. Jessie (Hollingsworth) Schipfer (1877-1956), wrote a piece about her family's move from Illinois entitled, "Jessie's Little Book." She wrote about her grandparents, Jeremiah and Catherine (Amos) Hollingsworth, who settled in Richland, Keokuk County, Iowa. Jeremiah was my 3rd great grand uncle. He purchased land and he and his wife raised their children in Richland, remaining there until their deaths. Jeremiah was one of the original signers of the Iowa Territorial Constitution.

I went in search of more pioneer stories about that particular area. I was entranced when I found Mary Ann's writings. The parallels of the Hollingsworths and Mary Ann's family were fascinating. Their families were so close geographically that it is certain they knew each other. In fact, Mary Ann married Benjamin Mills on October 15, 1849, in Richland, Iowa. Jeremiah's land, as well as that of his son Amos, was just adjacent to land owned by Charles Mills and Sarah Mills. Mary Ann had children of these names, but I am unsure whether it was her children's land or another Mills. Several other Mills owned land in the vicinity as well.

At the time of this writing, I have found just one marriage joining Mary Ann's family to a Hollingsworth. Mary Ann's great uncle, Jesse Embree, married my first cousin five times removed, Mary Hollingsworth. It is certainly a distant relationship in that it makes Mary Ann my first cousin (five times removed) of the wife of my first great uncle, but I am still quite pleased that we are "family." They would have all faced the same challenges living in Iowa Territory in those early days.

Mary Ann tells us that she has changed the names of some of the individuals in her story. She does not explain why, but undoubtedly it would have been for reasons of privacy, as many may have still been alive at the time of her writing.

Some of the content is not what we would consider acceptable in this day and age and may be seen as offensive. I have, none the less, left it as it was originally written. Words can be erased, but it is my belief they shouldn't be. How else to gauge our progress from where we've come, as well as how far we still have to go?

Mary Ann's relationship with the Indians is remarkable in that she had no fear even in some turbulent situations. She enjoyed playing with the Native American children at their camp and had Native American playmates. It is clear from her writing that those were the best days of her life and she deeply respected and admired the indigenous peoples who were her close neighbors.

Rachelle Tuttle, Editor

Prologue

Mary Ann Maulsby

Mary Ann Maulsby was born on June 6, 1830 near Greencastle, Putnam County, Indiana to John Cox and Sarah "Sally" (Moore) Maulsby. (Sarah will be referred to as "Sally" from this point forward, as that is the name Mary Ann uses.) She was just six years old when her family came to Iowa Territory, although it was still Wisconsin Territory until 1838. It is remarkable that she was able to remember so much about her early years.

John and Sally had six children, although a son, John, died in infancy in Iowa Territory. For reasons unknown, Mary Ann only speaks of one sibling other than John in her writing, a sister named Emily, even though other siblings were born in the same time frame. Mary Ann does not include other family members who lived nearby in her writing, either.

Mary Ann's maternal grandfather, Richard J. Moore, along with his sons Amos and Thaddeus, and her father John C. Maulsby, came to Iowa Territory in 1836 and took up claims in Washington County. Richard's claim was on section 33 and 34 of what is now Washington Township. They returned with their families in the fall along with Richard's wife, Rebecca (Embree) Moore, and children James Logan, Amos Embree, Thaddeus, William, Jesse, Richard Jr., Rebecca and Averila. Richard constructed a substantial log cabin.[1]

Mary Ann's father's land claim is said to be on section 29, which later became that of Michael W. Wilson.[2] It is adjacent to that of her grandfather Richard.

The first school in the township was in the kitchen of Richard and Rebecca's home. The first teacher was Mary Ann's great uncle John Embree.

---

[1] Portrait & Biographical Album of Washington County, IA, Acme Publishing Company, Chicago 1887.

[2] History of Washington County, 1880.

Richard J. Moore died on April 29, 1855 and Rebecca (Embree) Moore died on December 23, 1870 in Washington County, Iowa. They are both buried in the Moore Cemetery in Washington, Iowa.

Mary Ann's paternal grandparents were William (1774-1806) and Mary (Cox) Maulsby (1781- after 1806). Mary Ann's father was only about two years old when his father died. A second son, John's brother Thomas, was born in 1805, so he was only about a year old when his father died. I have not been able to ascertain when or where his mother passed away, but she is mentioned in William's will, probated in 1806, so sometime after that.

Mary Ann's mother Sally died on May 18, 1849 in Keokuk County when Mary Ann was just nineteen. Mary Ann married Benjamin Mills just a few months later. Sally's burial place is unknown, but is likely in the Friends Cemetery in Richland, IA.

Benjamin Mills

Benjamin Mills was born on February 12, 1829 in Lost Creek, Tennessee to John Mills and Mary "Polly" Janeway. He had five siblings: Lydia, Jane, Macy, Martha and Mary.

Benjamin's family came to Iowa Territory circa 1840 from Tennessee in a four-horse wagon overland to Keokuk County, Iowa, at a time when the settlements were so far apart that they had to go fifty miles to mill in order to secure flour.[3] They settled in Keokuk County, Iowa near Richland.

His mother died in Richland, Keokuk County, Iowa in the process of giving birth to Benjamin's sister Mary Annabelle on July 28, 1846. On August 31, 1847, his father married Rebecca (Hadley) Allen. Two children were born from this union; Benjamin's half-siblings Enos and John. His father died on November 10, 1853 in Jefferson County, Iowa. He is buried at the Friends Cemetery in Richland, Iowa. It is likely that Benjamin's mother is buried there as well, but her exact burial location is unknown.

---

[3] Past and Present of Hardin County, Iowa, Hon. William J. Moir, Editor, 1911

Children

Mary Ann and Benjamin had ten children together: Charles, Ira Thaddeus, Sarah Jane, John William, Mary Louise, Henry Maulsby, Macy J., Louis Benjamin, Ava Rilla and Martha Lodemia Mills. (See Genealogy, page 97). Their last-born child, Martha, known as "Demia," is to whom Mary Ann dictated her story.

Death and Burial

Mary Ann died on July 17, 1909 in New Providence, Hardin County, Iowa, having lived 79 years. Benjamin died November 21, 1897 in the same place at age 68. They are buried together in the Honey Creek Cemetery in New Providence.

Figure 1: Section 29 John Cox Maulsby claim; Sections 33 & 34, Richard Moore claim. An arrow points to Crooked Creek. Mary Ann refers to the Iowa River many times, but it would appear that what she believed to be the Iowa River was actually Crooked Creek, a tributary. Map: Page 151 of A.T. Andreas' Illustrated Historical Atlas of the State of Iowa. *(Chicago, Ill.: Andreas Atlas Co., 1875)*

Figure 2: Pioneers in Covered Wagon, *Thomas Fogarty. Image in the public domain.*

"When the pioneers of Washington County first made settlement within its borders, there was no railroad west of Chicago, nor was there even one reaching that city. Travel was made alone by ox or horse teams, most generally by the former, especially if long distances were to be traversed. To remove from the East required long and extensive preparations, and the journey was one of continual toil and anxiety, and even danger. The route lay through a wild and rough country; swamps and marshes were crossed with great exertion and fatigue; rivers were forded with difficulty and danger; nights were passed in the dense forests, with the earth for a couch and the trees and foliage for a shelter. Long weary days and weeks of travel were endured, but finally their eyes were gladdened and their hearts beat faster, when a vision of their future home burst upon them."

Portrait and Biographical Album of Washington County, Iowa, Brookhaven Press, 1887

1.

The Journey

Another Iowa blizzard! Well, I have seen many a one in this state and even before Iowa was a state, for I was here when Iowa was only a territory.

It was away back in the year of 1837 when John Maulsby, who was my father, came from his home in Green Castle, Indiana, bringing with him his wife and two little daughters, sister Emily and me, out here to Iowa Territory.[4]

Father was a true pioneer. He was afraid of no man or beast. He was born in east Tennessee when that state was new, when wild animals roamed through the forest. Indians, although they had been driven away south, were constantly returning and often their war whoop was heard in the forest. Many a cabin was left smoldering in its ashes as the Indians fled away with fresh scalps they had taken hanging from their belts.

After Father had grown to manhood he drifted to Ohio where he remained for a while and then he came on west to Green Castle, Indiana, where he managed a furniture and coffin shop. It was in Green Castle where he stole Sally Moore away from her parents and married her. I was born there on June 6, 1830.

But Father never did approve of closely settled countries. His kind was always following the Indians and wild things farther west. Sometime during his early young manhood, he had been out to Iowa which was then a wild territory where but few white men had ever been. So, Father knew the trail. He understood Indians, could speak several Indian languages and knew all their signs and customs.

When he decided to migrate to Iowa Territory, five or six other families decided to accompany him on this new venture. The first few days of our

---

[4] The Territory of Iowa was an organized incorporated territory of the United States that existed from July 4, 1838 until December 28, 1846, when the southeastern portion of the territory was admitted to the Union as the state of Iowa. The remainder of the territory would have no organized territorial government until the Minnesota Territory was organized on March 3, 1849. Source: Wikipedia.

journey toward the great wilderness was through Indiana, which at that time was quite thickly settled and we had reasonably good roads.

As we traveled on, the homes grew farther and farther apart. By the time we reached Illinois, the roads were only dim trails winding through underbrush and tall weeds. The oxen became worn out from pulling the wagons over soft ground and around rocks and logs of fallen trees that obstructed our way. We traveled on slowly from day to day, camping at night and cooking our meals over camp fires while the oxen rested and grazed on the grass and brush that grew along the way.

One evening we came to an old abandoned house. It stood back from the road, or what had at one time been a road. The cabin had been deserted so long that underbrush and weeds had grown up around it. Across the old road was a long stable and a well with a windless bucket and chain. Father, who always drove in the lead, had made up his mind to camp here and as he drove up to the place, he saw a man come out from the old log stable and disappear in the brush behind it.

Father knew the man. It was, well, I will not tell you his correct name for some of his people might hear about it and originate trouble. In fact, I will signify all those who came with us with assumed names except my own people. I will call the man "Wash Smith," who some eight or ten years ago had murdered Bill Stibbins in a drunken brawl which had taken place in the Green Castle Tavern. He then broke out of the jail and disappeared from Green Castle. Well, it seemed as though no one had seen him but Father and he said nothing to the others about it.

Soon the sun sank below the western horizon and after we had cooked our suppers over the camp fires, we made our beds inside the wagons. The camp was silent save the lowing of the cattle which were corralled nearby. Father, who could move as lightly and as silently as an Indian, slipped out of our wagon and walked around to the old cabin and cautiously tapped on the door. I heard Wash Smith softly unbar the door and Father passed inside and the door closed gently behind him.

When Father had gone from our wagon, I felt lonesome and afraid, for from somewhere out in the dark woods came a long, drawn out wailing of a wolf. I presume he was only howling at the moon but his wailing seemed to intensify the wild loneliness of the place.

Suddenly there came an agonized scream from among the cattle. Father rushed out of the old cabin, followed by Wash. "Stay back, Wash" I heard Father command in a low tone. I got out of bed and gazed out of the wagon and I saw by the moonlight that a panther had attacked a heifer and had ridden her down to death and already was making a gruesome supper of her remains.[5]

The rest of the cattle were bawling and milling around over the blood. Father ran to our wagon, seized his gun and with adroitness, shot the panther without any harm to the remainder of the cattle. But the camp was all aroused with excitement. Women and young girls who had hurriedly dressed in their homespun dresses and coarse cowhide shoes were clinging to their menfolks in the wild excitement and the men acted as though they were as badly frightened as the women and children.

"Now you can all go back to bed for all danger is passed," Father told them with a disgusted tone in his voice.

After quiet settled down over the camp, I heard Wash Smith come to our wagon and I heard Father say, "Well, Wash, if you are going to let your liquor alone, you might make your way out to the Iowa Territory where I am going. I think I will soon be going on alone, for this crowd that is with me will not hold out for long. They are too cowardly to endure the perils and hardships of a new country. You watch for them and after they pass here on their way back to Green Castle, you come to me in the wilderness where you can build a cabin and be safe from the law." I fell asleep then and heard no more.

The next evening our camping place was a site beside a small stream of water where we could get water for ourselves and our cattle. After we were all

---

[5] Mary Ann makes many references to panthers in her writing, but it is more likely that the animals were mountain lions. Other names often used: cougars, pumas, catamounts.

well established in our camp, two women took their buckets and started down to the creek to bring water. They were walking along when suddenly they screamed and came running back to the fire. They were so badly frightened they were unable to explain what they had seen.

Father walked down toward the stream of water and as he parted the bushes, he saw the gruesome bodies of two white men who had been murdered and scalped. Father said they had been dead several days for they were deteriorated beyond all recognition. Their clothes were rotted into shreds but there were still rotten cowhide boots upon the bones of their feet. There was nothing by which they could be identified, so Father came back to our wagon for his shovel and with the help of some of the men, dug a grave and buried them together. I presume their friends never knew what became of them.

The evening passed uneasily. The very stillness of the woods seemed threatening and sinister. The men stood around in groups discussing the incident and predicting what they believed would soon overtake themselves. Father was disgusted with them. I heard him say to Mother that he would be very glad if they all would get so frightened that they would turn their faces back toward Green Castle and leave him to go on alone with his family.

From Father's earliest childhood he had been used to tragedy and death of almost every description. He had often witnessed gruesome midnight orgies from which was sure to come some tragic death of brutality. With writhing horror, he had watched men die who were burning at the stake. He had seen hundreds of painted warriors coming home from the warpath with white men's scalps hanging from their belts on which the blood was not even dry.

He had seen many a desolate lodge that was filled with broken-hearted loved ones when some brave warrior who had fallen in battle was carried home by his comrades and laid down at the feet of his wife or sweetheart. To him, the sight of two dead men lying beside the trail in that Illinois wilderness was a very small event in comparison to what he had witnessed. He had no sympathy for such cowardice. It's no wonder that he lost patience with those people when they refused to go to bed and sat around the fire all night.

In our emigrant caravan there was a schoolmaster by the name of Westgate who claimed to have a call from God to go west and preach the gospel to the savages, as he called the Indians who lived in the Iowa Territory. Father had his doubts about God giving Westgate a call to go west and preach to those Indians, but anyway Westgate and his family were along.[6]

His wife was a frail, weak woman, but Westgate held to the idea that if he would answer the call of God, she would receive her healing. She constantly grew weaker until she couldn't get up at all but just lay on her bed in their wagon. At times she would scarcely recognize the women as they would climb in and out of the wagon doing all they could for her. Westgate, though, still had his mind on preaching the gospel to the heathens in the wilderness and believed his wife would soon get well.

Father knew that Westgate's wife would die, but there was nothing that he could do about it, for we were a long way from Green Castle and far from any help that one might receive from the Indians out in the wilderness.

When another day of traveling had passed and the men had driven their wagons close together in a small circle, Father went to the Westgate wagon. When he looked at Mrs. Westgate, he knew she was very close to death. Her face and limbs were so emaciated there was no flesh left on them and her eyes were glassy and had a strange expression. Father hastened to inform the women of the approaching crisis and they hurried to her wagon and did all they could for her, but it was of no use, for in a few moments she was dead.

All day the sky had been dark with a threatening cloud over the sun and now, even before our supper was cooked and eaten, the rain came down in torrents. Father cut down a large walnut tree and worked all night long in the rain hewing out boards and fashioning a coffin. The only light he had was a torch which he placed in a sheltered spot to keep the rain from extinguishing it.

---

[6] This was likely John Mosteller. Wife's name unknown. Source: History of Washington County, Iowa, From the First White Settlements to 1908 by Howard A. Burrell, Vol I, Copyright 1909 published by the S.J. Clarke Publishing Company

My little sister Emily and I had to stay all night alone in our wagon while Mother stayed with the Westgates. The next day Father placed Mrs. Westgate's body in the new walnut coffin which he had made and they buried her in a nice grassy place near an oak tree.

Now Mr. Westgate was through with his preaching the gospel to the savages in the wilderness. He was going back to Green Castle and most of the other emigrants were not long in making up their minds to go with him. They yoked their oxen to their wagons, drove out and started back along the trail they had made before the rain and soon disappeared from our sight.

Father was glad to see the last of them and the next morning we started on along toward the west. Now there was no road, not even a dim trail, but Father had an instinct when he was in the wilderness. Through that instinct he could make his own trail well, although there was nothing to direct him along. We drove on and on until we arrived at Ft. Armstrong and the man at the boat landing ferried us across the Mississippi River and we camped our first night on Iowa soil.[7]

---

[7] Fort Armstrong (1816–1836), was one of a chain of western frontier defenses which the United States erected after the War of 1812. It was named after John Armstrong, U.S Secretary of War under President James Madison. It was established May 10, 1816 by Colonel George Davenport and a work force of 600 soldiers and 150 laborers. It was located at the foot of Rock Island, in the Mississippi River near the present-day Quad Cities of Illinois and Iowa. It was five miles from the principal Sac and Meskwaki village on the Rock River in Illinois. In 1832, the U.S. Army used the fort as a military headquarters during the Black Hawk War.

Soon after the arrival of soldiers from the east in 1832, a local cholera epidemic broke out among the whites and Indians around Fort Armstrong. Within eight days, 189 people died and were buried on the island.

With the pacification of the Indian threat in Illinois, the U.S. Government ceased operations at Fort Armstrong and federal troops abandoned the frontier fort in 1836. It continued to be used by militia until 1845. The remains of the old fort were destroyed by fires in 1855 and 1859. A replica blockhouse was built in 1916. Source: Wikipedia and FortWiki.

Figure 3: Fort Armstrong replica blockhouse. Library of Congress, Prints and Photographs Division. Image in the public domain.

Figure 4: Fort Armstrong. Image in the public domain.

Figure 5: A Prairie Home. Source: A History of Keokuk County, Iowa. A History of the County, its Cities, Towns, Illustrated. *The Union Historical Company, Des Moines, 1880. Image in the public domain.*

2.

The Vision & The Loss of Baby John

The next morning Father yoked his oxen together and hitched them to the wagon and we started on.

"Sally, I had a vision last night," he said. "It impresses me in such a way I cannot shake it off. I dreamed that you and I were driving along in our wagon and you were holding in your arms a little white lamb. We were at the foot of a high bluff. I could see in my dream every tree and bush and there were vines hanging from the top of the trees to the ground. I could see the vines and the limbs of the trees swaying in the breeze and the wind was singing as it passed through them. All nature was happy and we, too, were happy, Sally - yes, you and I. Suddenly without warning our little lamb leaped from your arms and disappeared into the bushes. We hunted for him and we called for him to come back to us, but we never found him. Then the wind that had been singing through the treetops changed into mourning and the river which ran below us murmured and sighed. Even the wild things out in the forest cried out with grief because we had lost our little lamb."

He turned his eyes away from us so we could not see the tears that had gathered in them.

Mother did not believe so much in visions but she had lived with Father long enough to have some faith in what he would tell her; for many a time she had found that he understood these things and had told her the truth about them.

"Oh, John, why do you worry so much over nothing but a dream? Anyway, we have no lamb to lose, so why do you worry?" Mother replied.

I could see that she too was worried, and only talked in that way to hide her agitation. Father felt she didn't understand and he said no more.

He drove on toward the west with nothing to guide him but his forest instinct and the morning sun. We crossed sloughs and ditches where the oxen might have mired down and sometimes, we would come to a patch of timber growing along some stream of water and we would have to wind around to avoid the trees, underbrush, and fallen logs.

At last we reached the Iowa River and at the place where we forded the river was a beautiful spring of water that came dashing out from among the rocks. Mother pointed to a spot above the river at a level place on the side of a bluff.

"John," she said, "There is a nice place where we can build our cabin. There is plenty of wood here and we could get water from this spring for our household use."

"But Sally," he faltered, "this is the place where I dreamed we lost our little lamb."

"Oh, John," Mother exclaimed, feigning disgust, "that was only a dream. I like this place so well I want to build our cabin here." Father's handsome face fell, and his voice trembled a little when he answered her.

"Honey, I will build our cabin where you want it." Before the night had closed down, he was busy cutting down trees and trimming them up into logs for our cabin.

When the cabin was finished, Father, who had been a cabinet-maker in Green Castle, Indiana, began making our furniture. He made the two beds, table, and cupboard out of walnut, but he fashioned the chairs from hickory. Mother, who was an artist with a needle, made cushions and stuffed them with the feathers from the wild fowls that Father had shot for our meat.

After the cabin and furniture were finished, Father cut logs and built a stable with a heavy door and window shutters to keep out the big gray timber wolves and panthers that roamed around through the woods.

Life was hazardous in the Iowa Territory for cattle as well as it was for people. He made rails and fenced in a patch of ground so on warm days he could turn his oxen out to exercise in the sunshine.

We weren't settled very long in our new home until the Indians, who were camped nearby, came and brought us some beans, squash, cornmeal and salt. Even Chief Wishecomaque, who was the chief chosen by the Sac and Fox Nation that had refused to follow Chief Keokuk, came to our cabin to inquire if we had plenty of blankets to keep us warm through the cold winter that was fast approaching upon us.[8]

When the braves came in from off the chase, they brought us what they considered was our share of the meat. They also gave Father some lead for his gun and deer skins for our moccasins.

We were nicely settled in our new home when my little brother John was born. He was a very pretty baby and we were all very proud of him, but Father's face was sad and his eyes sometimes had a tragic look in them, for he seemed to have some dreadful presentiment concerning our baby. All too soon his dream came true, for we lost our little lamb. Father made a little coffin and laid him in it. He carried it out in the yard and set it on the ground. Soon there were fifteen hundred Indians gathered there.

The braves stacked their guns against the cabin wall. I never have seen so many guns in one place in all my life and perhaps I never will again. There were hundreds of guns that were stacked leaning against our little cabin. Chief Wishecomaque sat down on the ground beside the little coffin, then the others found places on the ground. Only a few braves remained standing and were leaning against the trees in the background.

Even yet, I can witness that scene, there were hundreds of those dark-faced people who were sitting there in that breathless silence on that beautiful day in October. The red leaves were falling around us and sometimes they would fall upon the little coffin. Young as I was, the immensity of that great wilderness bore down upon me as I listened to the sighing of the wind as it passed through the trees above me and the moaning of the river below me.

Chief Wishecomaque turned his face upward toward the heavens and prayed to the great spirit for the grief-stricken parents and for sister Emily and me. I could understand all he said for Father had taught me to understand and speak the Sac language. After the prayer, the forest people chanted a hymn. A brave gathered the little coffin in his arms and carried it to a grave that

---

[8] Chief Wishecomaque, "Hard Fish," became the chief of Black Hawk's village in Wapello County, where Eddyville now is. Source: Iowa History, an IAGenWeb Special Project.

someone had dug beneath a giant oak tree where they buried it. We saw our baby no more.

I know the forest people were shocked and surprised, for they could not understand why Father should put his helpless little child down into the ground instead of on a scaffold with food and water to give him a chance to gain the happy hunting ground, but they asked no questions. I know they felt sorry for us because we lost our little brother who might have grown up to be a great warrior and a mighty hunter.

Going back to the empty cabin was the hardest thing we had to do. Mother and Emily both cried so hard that Father had to take them in his arms and comfort them.

"Sally," he said, "I have been having a strange feeling about our baby. Now he will always be our baby. The girls will grow up and sometime leave home but our baby will never leave our home, for his spirit will always be with us and live in our hearts."

I did not cry but stood as stoic as stone. I felt as bad as the rest did but I knew that nothing in the world could bring our baby back to us so it was no use to cry.

After everything had settled down again and we all were feeling better, Father took my sister Emily and me on a long journey to the Des Moines River to see the great Chief Black Hawk.

Not long afterward the sky was overspread with cold, stormy clouds and a hard piercing wind blew angrily from the northwest, whistling and moaning among the naked branches of the trees. All too soon, the great forest was bleak, cheerless and choked with snow, and far up on the hillside above the frozen river we lived on in our little cabin, alone in that vast wilderness.

3.

The Girl That Floats

Spring came at last and the northwest wind that had been blowing with such vigor and bringing with its blasts hard stormy blizzards, had turned to the south and melted the snow. The trees and bushes were budding out and the robins had come back to live in Iowa Territory. The wilderness was alive again. The Iowa River was beautiful. Its water was clear and sparkling. Oh! If it could have remained as it was then.[9]

In my mind I can see it yet, deep and flowing swiftly within its banks, turning and bending upon itself. Its music in harmony with the birds singing above it. The shadows of the great trees reflecting in the water as it flowed on down to meet the Mississippi as God had created and intended for it to do.

Now, it is nothing but a ghost of itself, for the trees have mostly been cut down by the white man's ax and only a few remain that are growing along its water's edge. I presume the white man would have the audacity to plow up the moon and plant it to corn if it were possible. I thank God they can't do it, for the moon and the stars must remain as God created them.

The river, as well as the rest of the wilderness, is full of snares. I found this out late one evening while I was playing along the bank. I saw a place where there was evidence of some great struggle. The vines were torn from the boughs of a small tree. There were limbs of a sumac bent and broken and there was blood stain on last year's fallen leaves. I knew a panther had leaped down upon the back of a deer and had ravenously torn him to pieces and had made a feast on its remains. But that was only one wild thing of the wilderness preying upon another.

I turned and reached out into the river to fill my little bucket with water, when somehow, I lost my balance and slipped into the rushing, foaming river.

---

[9] This likely was not actually the Iowa River. It would've been Crooked Creek, a tributary to the Iowa River.

I had on my red riding cloak and hood that Mother had made for me out of waterproof material and as I had landed on my back, my cloak held me up so I floated down the river like a log.

Father had taught me to swim when I was four years old but the strongest man in the world would have had a hard time swimming in that raging current. After I had floated several rods down the river, the current carried me near the bank and I grabbed a sumac bush and pulled myself out of the water.

I was wet, cold and very muddy and my little bucket was lost in the river, but I made my way up the hill to the cabin. While Mother was helping me change my clothes, I cried because I had lost my little bucket, for I had brought it all the way from Green Castle, Indiana, and I valued it very much.

After this episode the Indians called me "The Girl That Floats." I don't know how they knew about the instance unless Rolling Thunder saw me and told them about it.

Rolling Thunder was a little Sac Indian boy. He was two years older than I, that is, when I was seven years old, he was nine corn plantings old. He could appear and disappear without making any noise. Sometimes I would be playing around and he would be no place in sight when suddenly he would be standing by my side just as if he had risen up out of the ground, his little moccasins making no more sound than his shadow. He always carried his bow and arrow and I never saw him without his little hatchet. I never knew him to kill a bird or a squirrel, but he was always taking aim at them, although he never would let his arrow fly.

Rolling Thunder had a wild beauty of speech that I enjoyed, especially when he talked of strange wild things that were hidden behind the hills. He would tell of the queer voices that came up from the river and told him things and what the wolves say when they howl at night. I liked him because he was always so happy and free from care. He had that freedom of the wilderness which made him a part of it. Young as he was, he understood the wilderness and all that was in it. I suppose it was Rolling Thunder who had seen me floating down the river and had told the other Indians about it.

All the next day the early spring clouds hung dark and heavy over the woods and the rain came down with a steady stream. Little rivulets came dashing down the side of the bluff and through our clearing, dodging the stumps on their way down to the river. Late in the evening a young Indian brave came to our cabin. It seemed as though he had been traveling all day through the woods, for his hunting shirt and his leggings were very wet and muddy. Cold rain was dripping from his scalp lock and running down his neck.[10] When he stepped into the cabin, water squashed from his moccasins, leaving a wet place on the cabin floor.

Father had sympathy for all kinds of people. To him, it mattered not what their condition was or whether their color was white, black or copper color, his latch string was always out to them, so the young brave remained in our cabin all night.[11] He took off his belt and hung his leggings and moccasins before the fireplace to dry. After wrapping himself in his blanket, he laid down on the floor to rest.

Several times during the night I heard him get up, reach for his leggings and moccasins and rub them for a while before hanging them back over the fire again. This he repeated several times in the night and when morning came, they were as dry and soft as if they had never been in the rain.

The next morning while we were eating our breakfast, Father, to tantalize the young Indian, filled a plate with bread, potatoes and squash and passed it to him, but immediately he handed it back to Father.

"White man no meat, white man no meat," he groaned with disgust. Father took his plate and placed a slice of venison on it and he sat back upon

---

[10] Most common with the Plains cultures, a scalp lock was a long lock of hair on the crown of the head, with the rest of the hair being shaved or cut. It was often decorated with beads and/or feathers. It held significant cultural and spiritual importance for some tribes. It could symbolize bravery, status or tribal affiliation. It could also be worn as a challenge to enemies.

[11] A cabin door's fastening consisted of a wooden latch catching on a wooden hook. To open the door from the outside, a strip of buckskin was tied to the latch and drawn through a hole a few inches above the latch-bar, so that upon pulling the string the latch was lifted from the catch or hook, and the door was opened. To lock the door, it was only necessary to pull the string through the hole to the inside. By keeping the latch string out, it meant that anyone was welcome to enter for shelter, sustenance or rest.

the floor and ate his breakfast. After the young Indian had finished his breakfast, he stood up and remained silent for a few moments.

"Good white man, good white man," he said and made his way out of the cabin and soon disappeared into the shadow of the woods.

This was only one of two instances when an Indian remained through the night in our little cabin, but they never slept in our beds. They would wrap themselves in their own blankets and lie on the cabin floor in front of the fireplace. They also never ate at our table, but they would sit on the floor and eat what Father would give them. Always taking their leave with that same remark: "Good white man, good white man." Quite often one would return with a gift of deer meat or wild fowl that he had chanced to shoot while wandering about through the woods.

Figure 6: Sac Indian Family 1899. Source: Library of Congress. F.A. Rinehart, photographer. Image in the public domain.

4.

Wash Smith

One night after the sun had gone down back of the bluff that loomed up behind our little cabin and the last glow had faded from the western sky and darkness had settled down over the woods, we were sitting around the fireplace with its bright polished andirons and its blazing back log when suddenly the wind rose and went blustering through the clearing. An owl perched on a limb above our cabin screeched out with a weird, mournful sound that ended in a long, drawn-out sinister chuckle. Somewhere far out in the woods a wolf threw back his head and sent out a long quivering wail. Instantly his wail was answered. He repeated the call and it was answered again and again.

"There is something strange and sinister out in the woods tonight, for that wolf is calling up a gang and the owls are all stirred up with their superstition and sending out their warning through the woods," Father remarked as he threw another log on the fire and the flames flashed up the chimney with a more homelike sound.

We had one window in our little cabin. Father had brought both the sash and glass all the way from Indiana. He got up from his chair, lighted another candle and placed it in the window. I didn't know why he did that but I knew Father understood this wilderness. He knew all its signs and secrets and we asked him no questions about his movements.

In the lull between the blasts of the wind we heard the faint cry of a white man in distress. It sounded weird and apprehensive out there in those dark woods. Father leaped from his chair and reached for his gun. It was then I realized what safety there was in that gun, not alone for himself, but for all of us who loved him and depended on him for our care and protection. He stuck his feet into his moccasins, ran out and disappeared into the blackness of the woods.

It was Wash Smith who was out there in the woods calling for help. He had come to Iowa Territory as Father had told him to do. Wash had been through many encounters with wild animals that roamed through the woods. Not so many in Illinois, for in eastern Illinois along almost any small creek or river he found a thin fringe of settlements where a parcel of land had been broken out and planted to grain. Even in the west part of Illinois there were a few scattered cabins where lived lone families who were seeking homes in the wilderness. Some of them were located on the very land that others had settled on before the famous Battle of Bad Axe had taken place, and had fallen prey to the tomahawk and scalping knife.[12] Wash had been welcome to stay all night at any one of these cabins that he would be near when night overtook him.

In Iowa Territory that year of 1837 there were not more than ten thousand people throughout the entire region and they lived mostly in Dubuque and Des Moines counties, or what now are counties.

After Wash Smith had crossed the Mississippi River, his difficulties began. He had lived on roots and nuts he found in the woods and a little parched corn he had left in his pocket. It had been very hard for him to find the way to the Iowa River and several times he had fought with wolves. One night when he had fallen asleep and let his fire die down, they had attacked him. After shooting at them until his ammunition was all gone, he ran to a tree which he climbed and remained there the rest of the night.

He reached the Iowa River at last and while he was following the Indian trail down the river looking for our cabin, he glanced behind him and saw a large panther step out of the bushes onto the trail and soon, to his dismay, he realized the carnivorous feline was following him. When Wash would stop walking, the panther would stop and remain quiet. When Wash would gaze at him, he would sit down and turn his head in the opposite direction, but when

---

[12] The Bad Axe Massacre was a massacre of Sac (Sauk) and Fox Indians by United States Army regulars and militia that occurred on August 1–2, 1832. This final scene of the Black Hawk War took place near present-day Victory, Wisconsin. It marked the end of the war between white settlers and militia in Illinois and Michigan Territory, and the Sac and Fox tribes under warrior Black Hawk. Source: Wikipedia.

Wash would walk on again, the panther would get up and follow, keeping a certain distance behind him.

It was now getting dark and as Wash had no more ammunition for his gun, he became greatly alarmed but kept on walking down the trail, for there was really nothing else he could do. Soon he came to a pile of rails that Father had made for more fencing. Keeping his eyes on the panther, Wash walked backward until he came up to the rails, then he began building a pen around himself.

As the darkness thickened, the panther came closer and began a circuitous route around the rail pen, closing in faster and faster as he made the rounds. Wash saw the light from the candle through a gap in the trees that Father had placed in the window of our cabin and he began calling for help.

Father was not afraid of wild animals for he understood them, and too, he had a look of mastery about him to cause all who knew him to honor him and follow his leadings. Even the wildlife of the forest seemed to sense his superior intelligence and left him alone.

It was only a few evenings before this occurred that Father was walking along through the woods carrying his broad ax upon his shoulder when he saw a large panther before him and directly in his path. He was standing with both his front feet upon a log and gazing around. Father came on down the path without giving back an inch and neither did the panther give back an inch. Father looked at the panther but the big cat could not meet his eyes and turned his own eyes away.

Father never took life without a reason and neither of them was afraid of the other, so they each went their way. Had the panther attacked Father he would have crushed his skull with his broad ax.

The panther that followed Wash Smith was not attending to his own business so he deserved to die. As Father approached the rail pen, the ravenous cat leaped upward with his great paws extending in the air, but a bullet met him half way and went crushing through his brain. He fell backward quivering in death upon the ground.

It was getting quite dark out there in the shadow of the woods. It was so dark Father could scarcely see the man inside the rail pen, but when Wash spoke, Father recognized him immediately and they walked together up the hillside to our little cabin. Father pulled the latchstring and the heavy door swung open. They stepped inside and Father shut the door, drew the bar across it and it clinked into place.

Father took Wash's coonskin cap and hung it on a wooden peg that had been driven into the log wall and placed his gun alongside his own in the corner of the cabin. "You can stay here with us, Wash," Father said. "I will help you build a cabin of your own. We have no sheriff, judge or jury out here in this wilderness and you are safe from the law for a few years at least."

"I don't like the wild animals and snakes you have here, but I know I must remain here, for if I go back to Green Castle it will only mean death. Sometimes I think a fellow would be better off to die for a crime than to live and bear the burden of it and always be running from the law."

Wash talked on, "I can see why such men as myself and that ignorant class of people who have no place in the world or who know nothing of civilized life should come out here and expose themselves to the wild animals and snakes, but I can't understand why a man like you with your education and ability would want to come out here and live among these dirty redskins in the God-forsaken wilderness. You could, with your manners and speech, get along in any large city or small town and enjoy the very best of society that civilization has to give. In fact, you gave up a good paying business to come out here."

"There is a lure about this wilderness that gets into one's blood," Father answered him. "It fascinates and draws and holds one like me. It is true there are cats and wolves out here in the wilderness but there are cats and wolves in the city too. Wolves in sheep's clothing, while out here they are just plain wolves. They are not deceiving anyone, and if you understand the wild animals, you can get along with them. The wilderness is for those who know it and can see the hand of God in its creating."

The logs in the fireplace crackled and flamed and threw out a cheerful light and warmth in the little cabin. The wind came shrieking down the chimney, then toned down into a sob and sigh to intensify the loneliness of the great wilderness. The little owl that was perched on a limb above the little cabin again screeched out his sinister chuckle and far out in the dense woods the wolf again sent out his long quivering wail.

"Listen to that heavenly music," Father exclaimed.

"I don't hear anything but that blasted, gol darn wolf a-howling," Wash answered after listening intently for an instant. "I feel as if I will never be able to get my mind off of that panther. I will live that gol darn deal over many times in my dreams."

"You will soon get accustomed to these wild things that live out here," Father said as he commenced making preparations for bed, and soon quiet settled down inside the little cabin.

Figure 7: The New Home. Genevieve Foster, 1939. Library of Congress. Image in the public domain.

Figure 8: Indian village

Figure 9: Indian village. Image in the public domain.

5

Fun at the Indian Camp

Mother was so timid and afraid she seldom left the cabin unless Father was with her. She was afraid of the Indians, panthers, wolves and snakes. She was afraid for Emily too, and never allowed her to play outside. The only time that I had the audacity to talk back to her was once when she tried to keep me inside the cabin, too.

I can recall the scene now. We had just finished our noonday lunch and Father was getting ready to go back to his work in the woods. I was making preparations to accompany him when Mother gazed at me and exclaimed, "Mary Ann, you are not going to the woods this afternoon. You are going to stay inside and help me with the housework."

"But I must help my father with his work," I protested. "For he needs me."

"I need your help with the housework, too," she answered with agitation in her voice.

"You have Emily," I suggested.

"Emily is too little to be of any help," she said, then turned and appealed to Father who was standing beside the fireplace and leaning against the mantel.

"John, why shouldn't Mary Ann stay inside?" she asked him. "She just runs around through the woods, penetrating the thickets just like a young catamount, tearing her clothes off herself, and soon some wild beast will tear her to pieces and devour her just as they would a young deer."[13]

"The wild animals will not harm Mary Ann," Father answered, laughing as he said, "They look upon her as the old Greek mythology would call a wood nymph of the hills, and they will let her alone."

"But now she is old enough to learn to sew and do housework. Do you want her to just grow up out here among the Indians in this wilderness like

---

[13] A medium-sized or large wild cat, especially a cougar.

underbrush and never know anything?" she asked him, but as usual when Father didn't want to say anything when he was questioned, he withdrew behind that barrier of remoteness which he possessed and said nothing.

"Father needs me," I repeated. "I am all the help he has and I will not forsake him. You don't treat Father right," I continued. "You could be more of a companion and help to him if you would. There is no need of your being so afraid of everything, for nothing could harm you while you are with him, but you won't go with him, nor will you let Emily go. I am all the help he has while he is working so hard to build us a home in this beautiful place, and I will not leave him to work alone."

Mother looked frightened and soon began to cry. Father said nothing but he stood there with a peculiar expression written on his face. It was one I could not analyze and I turned and ran out of the cabin. What passed between them after I left, I never knew but soon Mother called me. When I came inside, I saw her face and eyes were swollen from much weeping. I knew it was wrong for a seven-year-old girl to talk like that to her mother but I knew too that what I had said was the truth, so I made no apology.

"Mary Ann, I am going up the river with your father in the boat," she said with a catch in her voice. "Now you must stay here inside the cabin with Emily while I am gone and be sure you keep the door barred. Don't unbar the door for any reason, no matter what happens," she admonished with emphasis.

I said nothing but I watched out of the window and when their boat disappeared from my sight, I took Emily by the hand and ran down to the Indian camp. Emily was a very pretty little girl and Mother always kept her hair washed and curled. Her clothes were always clean, for Mother would make her sit still in her little chair so her clothes would stay clean.

When Father was up to Dubuque, he had gotten Emily a pair of little red Morocco shoes which made her appear all the more dainty, but I felt sorry for her. She had never been to the Indian camp, nor ever played with the Indian children. I had promised her the first time I had a chance to get her away from Mother I would take her down there.

I loved to be at that Indian camp, for everything there seemed so wild and free. In fact, everything around there was free and happy. Above the lodges were the birds singing and chattering around among the branches of the great ancient oaks and the leaves fluttering in the cool spring breezes. Below was the beautiful Iowa River with its waves as wild and free from care as those other wild things of nature.

I loved to run and play ball and play at scalping the whites with those Indian children, and now at last my little sister was sitting here among them with her pretty dark curls tossing about in the wind. The Indians gathered around her and I believed they had never seen anyone before who had curly hair, for they would feel her hair and stick their fingers inside a curl and laugh and talk about her and exclaim how pretty she was.

One old woman kept shaking her head, groaning and murmuring words I could not understand. I asked Rolling Thunder what she was saying. He said, "She says, 'girl that floats' little sister too pale, soon die, need more sunshine."

Emily could not understand what they were saying. She became badly frightened and stayed close to me until one of the women gave her a lump of maple sugar to eat, then she knew they meant to be friendly and would not do her any harm.

That spring when they made their sugar, they borrowed Mother's big wash kettle to boil the sap down in and when they returned the kettle, they brought a bucket of sugar and gave it to us so we too had plenty of good sugar. When I say "bucket," I mean a wooden bucket with iron hoops, for we had no pails in those days -- they were all buckets.

The way some people talk about the Indians, I suppose if one didn't know them, they would have been afraid to use that sugar for fear it might be dirty, but we knew their sugar was clean. I have often heard people make remarks about the dirty Indians with their dirty wigwams full of flies. That is a great mistake, for the Indians that I knew were not dirty. They bathed and washed their clothes in the river and if a lodge or wigwam got dirty or polluted with disease, they would burn it down and build another out of new material on clean ground.

And flies? Why, the Indians had no flies. It was the white people who brought the flies. Bees came just before civilization, but flies came after. When we came to Iowa Territory there were plenty of bees. All we had to do when we wanted honey was to find a bee tree and gather the honey. We had no flies in our cabin until several years after the white settlers came in.

The Indians had several little puppies running around the camp and while we were there, they filled one of their sugar troughs with water and put the puppies into the trough so Emily could see how they could swim. It sure was fun to see them swim and splash around in the water, for they were so fat and squabby.

We were having a good time when I happened to glance up the river and saw my father's boat coming around the bend. Immediately I took Emily's hand and we ran to our cabin. I was sure I would be found out, for Emily couldn't run very fast for her legs were too short. We had just reached home and ran inside when they came near enough to see what was going on around the cabin.

They never knew I had taken Emily to the Indian camp. I never told them and Emily knew if she told she would be severely punished. She was more afraid of what I would do to her if she told than she was of the punishment she would receive from Mother. Also, she knew I would never take her to the Indian camp again if she told on me and got me into trouble.

6

Popacrack and Cassie Casteel

I can thoroughly understand how the psalmist was feeling when he said, "I will lift up mine eyes unto the hills from whence cometh my help." I suppose the great King David was thinking of the temple that stood on a hill in Jerusalem where he sometimes went to worship when he made that remark, but when I was a child, I needed no temple to worship in. I could worship on the hills without a temple. They made me think of our creator who was here before the world was.

I loved the hills. In fact, I loved everything about the wilderness. It was home to me and I, too, was a part of it. I loved its mystery, its vastness. Even a wolf, like a gray shadow coming down the Indian trail, or a deer with its great pleading eyes and trim limbs leaping away into the shadow of the great forest trees, had their places in this great wilderness. Oh, it was wonderful to have a cabin here and be a part of this great creation. It has meant more to me than all the civilization that life has ever held for me.

One evening as I was sitting quietly gazing out of the window at the hills, to my surprise I saw, through a gap in the trees, two horsemen coming slowly down the Indian trail. When I mentioned seeing them, Mother and Emily ran to the window and eagerly searched the line of hills with their eyes. They saw nothing because the riders had then disappeared behind a cluster of trees. "It is only your imagination that has conjured up two riders," Mother exclaimed with disgust in her voice as she went back to her chair.

I knew I had seen them and I kept watching and soon they came into sight again. They came on and rode up into our clearing, dismounted and tied their horses to the fence and came into the cabin. They were a man, a woman and a baby. As mother remarked afterward, the man looked like a horse thief. His face was covered with a long black beard. His hair was black and grizzled with gray about his temples. He had a bad looking scar across the side of his face, extending downward to his neck. It looked as though he had sometime been slashed with a sharp knife.

I didn't like the expression in his gray eyes, for they were ugly and reminded me of a snake. He was slouchy and slovenly. His shirt had two or three holes in it and the collar was torn clear off and gone and only a part of the neckband remained. He wore a pair of cowhide boots that were drawn up over the legs of his faded jean trousers.

The woman was a tall, bony, manish-looking person. She had on a dark blue homemade dress, a pink calico sun bonnet and a plaid shawl, and if she had ridden into our clearing a straddle a broomstick, instead of a horse, she could easily have passed for a witch. Even the baby appeared more like some little hobgoblin than a human child.

They introduced themselves to Mother as Popacrack and Cassy Casteel and said they had come all the way from Ohio. They asked the privilege to stay all night in our cabin. Mother told them they were welcome to stay.

After the formality of meeting these strange people, Mother knelt down in front of the fireplace, raked the ashes from off the coals and held a stick of pitch pine against them until it caught and blazed up. She threw on some dry wood and placed a kettle of deer meat over the fire to cook. It was still early spring and as the strangers had ridden far that day, they were chilled through. They drew their chairs up to the fire to warm themselves and the baby.

Father came home from his work and we had our supper and soon the night closed down. Since Father had helped Wash Smith build a cabin and Wash had gone to live in it, Mother arranged the bed in which Wash had slept while he was staying at our cabin for the Casteels. They were very tired and went to bed early.

The next morning while Mother was getting breakfast, for some reason the Casteels began quarreling. I don't remember now what it was about. Mr. Casteel was sitting on a chair tilted back against the wall and was holding the baby on his knees. Mrs. Casteel became very angry and reaching out to the fireplace, grabbed the tongs and made a pass at Pop's head with them.

Pop succeeded in dodging the blow and jumping from his chair. He held the baby in front of him to protect his face from the blows. Mother sprang forward screaming frantically, "Stop, you'll kill your baby! Stop, you'll kill your baby!" Cassy changed her maneuvering and began larruping him around his legs just below where he was holding the baby.

Pop danced around on the puncheon floor, first on one foot, then on the other in trying to dodge the violent blows.[14] I know his legs must have turned black and blue and perhaps bleeding from the severe mauling which his wife had given them. Anyway, I noticed he was limping for several days afterward.

This was interesting fun for us children but it was tragedy for Mother, who was not strong and was too nervous to endure such an exhibition as the Casteels put on that morning.

When we told Father about the way they had acted, he said, "Well, they say that men invented hell but it looks as though it is the women who keep the fires burning. I will go and get Wash Smith to help me build a cabin for them and in that way, we can get rid of them."

When Wash Smith saw Mrs. Casteel, he knew her. He said he had been acquainted with her in Ohio and that sometime before she had married Popacrack Casteel, she had met a free Negro who was the owner of a fine team of black horses. She had married him with the intention of taking him south where she could sell him into slavery, then she would return again to Ohio, bringing with her the team of fancy horses and the money which she hoped to realize from the sale of the Negro.

After her marriage to the Negro, she told him they would ride the horses south on a honeymoon trip and visit some of her relatives, but at the first place they stopped to stay all night on their way south, she did not treat him as he felt a new husband should be treated. He noticed that she introduced him as her boy instead of her husband. During slave times all Negro slaves were introduced as the owner's "boy" no matter how old the Negro might be.

---

[14] Puncheons are logs that are flattened on one side only.

When night came, the people where they stayed put the Negro to sleep in the stable with the horses while Cassy occupied a room in the house. It was then the Negro understood her intentions, but he said nothing that night. The next day after traveling awhile toward the south, he suddenly and without any warning jerked her off of his horse and after giving her a terrible beating, took his horses and started back toward his home in Ohio. He left Cassy sitting alone beside the road. How she made her way back to Ohio, Wash did not know, for he said he had never heard of her again until he saw her that morning in our cabin here in Iowa Territory.

The next evening when Father came home from the woods where he had been working, getting out logs for the Casteel cabin, he saw that Mother was so nervous and upset that she actually was sick. He took her in his boat and rode up the river to a quiet place where she would be alone and rest. Sister Emily and I were left alone with the Casteels.

It was along about seven o'clock that evening that I was standing in the door of our cabin, gazing at the scene around me, when I saw a black cloud coming up from the southwest. A streak of lightning then flashed across the sky followed by a low rumble of thunder and I knew a storm was approaching. I stood there looking up into the sky. Somehow, I loved a storm. I hadn't yet learned to be afraid of lightning and I liked to watch it flash across the sky and listen for the wild roll of thunder that was sure to follow. To me then a storm was just another wild thing that belonged to the wilderness.

Suddenly the lightning struck a tree not far from the cabin and tore out a big slab that came crashing to the ground. With a shriek like all the demons in existence were turned loose, the wind whirled itself upon us and soon our little clearing was enveloped with a furious storm of wind and rain.

When I slammed the door shut, I heard a sob and looking around, I saw Pop Casteel on his knees by the side of a chair in the attitude of prayer. I thought it very strange that he would become so concerned about his soul just at a time like this. He grew louder in his supplications and I could hear what he was saying.

"Oh Lord, deliver me from this terrible, furious storm which thou has sent upon us, and you know Lord that thou hast said in thy written word in the Bible that every tub must stand upon its own bottom. Now Lord save me and if every tub must stand on its own bottom, then that means if Cassy is delivered from this infernal storm, she will have to pray for herself. Amen."

Father had taught me to read when he was around (although I was only seven years old), and he helped me with the hard words I was reading in the Bible. I knew what Pop Casteel had said about every tub standing on its own bottom wasn't in the Bible. I knew it was just an old saying. Then there was the baby who was too young to know how to pray. If Pop must pray for himself or be blown away, and if Cassy must pray for herself or take the consequence, then who would pray for the baby? Surely they would not leave the baby to be blown away for the lack of prayer, but the wind grew calm and the rain passed on and no one was blown away, not even Cassy, who was too stubborn and contrary to pray.

Soon Father and Mother came home from their boat ride up the river and we were all safe at home in our little cabin once again.

7

Snakes

We live such narrow lives in this time which we call civilization. We get up at a certain time in the morning and proceed with our tasks through the day the same as we did yesterday and the same as we will tomorrow and the next day, and the next, and the same all through the year, and the next year -- it is the same on and on and on until we are gathered to our graves, and what have we done? Or what have we accomplished? Nothing different from the general trend of things.

In the wilderness we had food for our mind development, as well as for our bodies. Every day we had some new adventure, some new problem to confront. Every day we had a little more accomplished until a new and comfortable home loomed up before us that we had succeeded in wrenching from the heart of the forest.

It is true, we had snakes to contend with, but they were the kind of snakes that had principle enough to warn us with a rattle before they would strike. In this time when people pride themselves with what they call "civilization," we have human snakes; yes, human snakes in the grass to deal with who strike without warning and without giving us a chance to defend ourselves.

One day in the early spring, I was playing along the river and I saw on the opposite bank what at first I thought was a big rock. As I had not noticed it there before, I watched it and soon I saw it move slightly, then to my surprise, I saw it was a great ball of snakes. They had worked themselves out of a large hole that extended far back into the bluff above the river. Soon they began to loosen and as one would loosen from the ball, it would roll down into the river below.

When I ran and told Father, he took his gun and we sat together on a log on the opposite bank from them and he shot at them as they rolled down.

He must have shot a hundred or more and they were washed away down the river.

That summer there were Yellow Timber Rattlers everywhere. They were under the cabin floor, under the log door step and in the path that led from the cabin to our log stable. As I would walk down the hill through the woods to the spring for a bucket of water, they would be coiled in the path before me.

Father cut a pole of a size that I could handle well that I called my snake pole. He taught me how to strike to paralyze them with the first blow. There is a system in killing poisonous snakes, as well as anything else we have to do, and if one meddles with them and doesn't want to get stung, he had better adhere to that system.

I never was bit by one nor did I ever let one get away that I had come in close contact with. Wherever I went, if it was to the spring for a bucket of water, or on some errand which took me through the woods, or if I was just playing around about the clearing, I usually had my snake pole in my hand. Then too, our dog was quite efficient at killing snakes.

When he came upon one which was coiled and ready to strike, he would run around it in a circle keeping at a distance beyond its reach as it would spring to strike. He would keep on worrying it until the snake would become weary and start to crawl away, then he would seize it by the back of its neck and shake it until it was crushed, helpless and dying. I never knew him to get bit, for he was always on the lookout for them and he was too wise a dog to give them any advantage.

The largest snake I ever killed, and the time when I came close to getting stung, was once when I was on my way to the spring to bring a bucket of water. The ground on either side of the path that lead from our cabin to the spring was covered with trees, thick brush and tall weeds. I was walking along the path when I heard a well-known rattle. I cautiously parted the brush and glanced through the gap and there lay coiled the largest timber rattler I had ever seen.

It was brilliantly spotted and was loosely coiled with its great head uplifted and weaving from side to side. Without hesitation the big reptile sprang forward. Dropping my water bucket, I succeeded in dodging the deadly blow and before he had time to coil again, I struck with all the strength I had, just as my father had taught me to strike, breaking its back with the first effort and the rest was easy.

I gathered up my bucket, filled it with water and made my way back to the cabin. I didn't say anything about this experience to Mother for she was always so nervous and afraid I knew it was best to keep the encounters I had with snakes to myself. Both Father and I had many encounters with the wild creatures in the forest that we did not tell her.

One day when Mother was preparing our noon lunch, she opened the cupboard door and there lay a timber rattler coiled among the dishes. How he got there we never knew unless he had crawled in at the door, for Father had built the cabin strong and tight and there were no cracks through which a snake could crawl. He must have come in at the door or through the window which had been left open to admit the air. I wanted to get him out myself but Mother was so badly frightened she would not let me try. My birthday had been in June and now I was eight years old, and I felt as though I was almost grown up and quite capable, and I knew I could get him out if she would let me try; but no, I must wait until Father came home. He got him out and killed him.

Mother was so frightened and sick she could do no more so Father and I took all the dishes out of the cupboard, scoured the cupboard shelves, washed the dishes and placed them back again and finished preparing the noon lunch. When Mother arose from her chair to take her place at the table, she began to stagger, "Oh, I am so sick and everything is whirling around." she exclaimed. Father caught her as she fell and laid her gently upon the bed. There was a cup of water on the table and he sprinkled some of it on her face and moistened her lips.

Father always had a great deal of sympathy and understanding for her. He did not go to work that afternoon but sat by her bed to comfort her. I too, felt sorry for her, for she looked so pale and exhausted. Although I couldn't understand why one should get so sick over nothing but a snake, for both the cupboard and dishes were clean, since Father and I had washed them as they were before the snake had been in them. If he had crawled out before Mother had seen him, she would never have known he had been there and would not have gotten sick.

When I saw her lying there looking so pale among the white pillows, I thought of what Father had said once when I had complained to him about her being afraid.

"She is a flower, Mary Ann, a rose that should be tended and cared for in a quiet, comfortable home and surrounded by every luxury, and not out here in these wild woods where you and I belong." I was very proud of our new cabin and I could not understand why it was not comfortable enough for any one, but I never questioned anything Father said so I let it go at that. I never could understand her nor did she ever understand me.

When we killed a snake anywhere around the cabin, we would put it in an old stump that stood some distance from our clearing so we would not injure our feet by stepping on the bones after it decayed.

One day after I had killed a snake and put it into the old stump, I saw another just like the one I had killed come to the old stump and began to roll its dead mate out upon the ground. He did not get very far in his efforts until he received a crushing blow from my snake pole. I laid him to rest beside his companion in the old stump.

One afternoon when both Wash Smith and Pop Casteel were at our place, they were sitting on our log doorstep when they saw a snake crawling around the yard. Wash rose from the step, went out to a hickory tree and cut a forked stick with his pocket knife. For his own amusement he began teasing the snake by holding it down with the hickory stick. He placed the fork of the stick just back of the snake's head and when he would push down on the stick the snake's mouth would fly open. Pop Casteel hastily took from his pocket a pouch of tobacco, and after pulverizing it in his mouth for a moment, spit some of the juice into the snake's mouth. Immediately the snake became very sick and soon flounced over on his back where he lay for a few minutes and then died.

These are only a few of the many experiences we had with the snakes while we were living in the new Iowa Territory.

Figure 10: Indian boy

8

Slow Horse and the Little Silver Pipe

In the Indian camp there lived a little two-year-old boy whom they called "Slow Horse." His name wasn't very appropriate for him. If his name had to be "Horse" at all, it should have been "Fast Horse," for he could run very fast on his little chubby legs.

The little Indian children are usually shy with white people but little Slow Horse was always friendly with both Father and me. He had a little silver pipe that was about the size of a lady's sewing thimble. He thought a great deal of his little pipe and whenever I would go down to the camp he would run and get it and bring it to me. My father was a prophet and could see and know what would take place in the future. A strange, transient change would come over his countenance when he would be playing with little Slow Horse. I knew Father looked like something dreadful was sure to follow.

Soon little Slow Horse was taken sick and after the Indian women had done all they could for him, they sent for the medicine man but he steadily grew worse. They came to our cabin and requested Father to come and see if he could do anything for him. Father knew it would be of no use but he went and succeeded in easing his suffering to a degree, but babies die everywhere both in the woods and in what people call civilization. In the night we heard a strange sound. It was the wild wailing of the Indian women and we knew that little Slow Horse was dead.

Mother didn't like Indians and she was disgusted with their wailing. She said they reminded her of a herd of cattle bawling over blood. I remembered how she cried when our baby died and I knew an Indian mother has the same feeling for her baby as a white woman has. My father had sympathy for Indians, as well as he did for white people, and when he heard the wailing, he got up from his bed, put on his clothes and went down to the camp and did all he could for them.

The next day he made a little coffin like the one he made for our baby and took it down to them. After the Indian women had washed and dressed the little fellow, or as it actually was, wrapped him in his blanket, they laid him in the coffin. The Indians placed his little silver pipe in his hand.

They conducted the funeral services very much the same as they did for our baby. The Chief took his place beside the coffin and after a time began speaking. The sound of his voice comes back to me now. There was both sorrow and cadence in it.

He spoke of the whispering of the wind, the murmuring of the river and how all nature worships our great creator. The people then chanted a hymn. They meant it for a death song but to me it was more like a life song, for it was about the beautiful hunting ground where little Slow Horse was now on his way to dwell. The Chief finished the services with a prayer. Instead of burying the coffin in the ground, they tied it to the limb of a tree and hung beside it a small bucket of soup, a gourd filled with water and a bundle of the baby's clothing.

In those days if an Indian committed a crime the other Indians would punish him. If the crime was very bad, they would put him to death. Just a little while before Slow Horse died, they had tomahawked an Indian and had buried him deep down in the ground. Father asked them why they didn't put him on a scaffold, or in a tree, like they did the baby. They said the man was a mean Indian and would go to the dark region below anyway, so they might as well bury him in the ground as to go to the trouble of putting him on a scaffold. But Slow Horse was an innocent little child that had never done any harm to anyone and it was their duty to help him along toward the great spirit so they buried him up instead of down.

After a time when the Indians knew that little Slow Horse had finished his long journey to the great spirit, they took the bucket of soup, the gourd of water and the bundle of clothing down from the tree, but they left the little coffin hanging there on the limb.

"Father, why did little Slow Horse have to die?" I asked. "He was the best little fellow in the whole camp. If death must come to them, why couldn't some of the others have died instead of him?"

"Mary Ann, the white settlers will soon be pouring into Iowa Territory like a rushing, whirling river spreading and submerging all that oppose them. After they have filled in here, they will roll on and on farther west driving the Indians ahead of them. They will cut down the trees, shoot off the deer until there will be no more wilderness left. Then where will the Indians stay and how will they live? Can't you see and understand the hard time Slow Horse would have had if he had remained here? The great spirit knows all things so he took the little fellow to himself."

"Will the great spirit take Rolling Thunder away, too?" I asked.

"No, the great spirit will not take Rolling Thunder away, for he has a great mission for Rolling Thunder," he answered. "Someday he will become a great chief and he must lead his people, and if possible, bring them out of their trouble and their chaotic condition."

Every summer when the corn was knee high the Indians would lay their corn by and some would go to the lead mines to mine lead.[15] Others would start fishing, while there were others who would gather flags to make mats and baskets. The young braves would go out on the chase. Sometimes they would be gone a week and sometimes a month would pass before they would return to their camp.

I had a grapevine swing in the woods not far from the tree in which little Slow Horse was buried. One day while the Indians were away, I grew tired of swinging and wandered down past there and to my surprise and horror, the little coffin was on the ground. The lid was off and the body was lying a little way from it. I ran and told Father and he hastened along with me to the tree. When he saw what had happened, he sent me back to our log stable to bring his spade. We dug a grave and placed the little body back in the coffin.

---

[15] The process involving cultivating the soil around the base of the corn plant to remove weeds and create mounded rows or ridges, which helps to conserve moisture, control weeds, and provide support to the growing plants.

We then hunted and searched the ground over for his little silver pipe, but we did not find it and we had to bury him in the ground without it. I felt very badly about it.

"Father, when little Slow Horse wakes up on resurrection morning and comes up out of his little grave, do you think he will miss his little silver pipe?" I asked. "Mary Ann, I don't suppose the little fellow will be thinking very much about his playthings at a time like that," he answered.

Afterward I knew that old Pop Casteel had stolen the little silver pipe. I saw him with it in his possession and I told Father that I believed that old Pop had cut the rawhide strings, instead of the squirrels chewing them like we had at first supposed, and let the little coffin fall so he could steal the pipe. I never liked Pop Casteel and now I despised him, for I believed any man who was so mean and cowardly enough to steal from a little helpless dead child would do anything, however bad it might be.

I thought how if the Indians were to see him with that little silver pipe, they might tie him to a post and set fire to him and I felt it would only serve him right if they did.

When the Indians came home again, Father and I walked down to the camp and told them what had happened and what we had done. After standing for several minutes silently gazing down at the little mound, they spoke and said, "Good white man, good white man."

That's when we knew we had done what was right.

Figure 11: Indian burial scaffolds. Image in the public domain.

Figure 12: Mountain lion waiting to pounce.

In 1840 Dr. Isaac Galland noted a large number of fauna in Iowa, including bison, elk, deer (either white-tailed deer or mule deer), raccoon, fox squirrel, mountain lion, lynx, gray wolf, black wolf, coyote (he called them prairie wolves), bear, beaver, otter, muskrat, mink, rabbits (presumably cottontail rabbit and hare), opossum, skunk, porcupine, groundhog, timber rattlesnake, prairie rattlesnake, bull snake, black snake, water moccasin, garter snake, water snakes, turkey, prairie chicken, quail, swan, geese, brant goose, duck, crane (he called them pelicans), crow, blackbird, bald eagle, "grey eagle" (probably a hawk or falcon), buzzard, raven, mourning dove, passenger pigeon, woodpeckers, woodcocks, hummingbird, and the honeybee.

Source: Wikipedia; Environment of Iowa.

9.

Fierce Wild Beasts

In those days deer could be seen daily, trooping through the woods in droves from twelve to twenty and sometimes as many as fifty would be seen grazing together. Quite often a few would wander into our little clearing and if we were very quiet inside the cabin they would come near the door in their reconnoitering around. If we made the slightest noise, though, they would go bounding away like they were sailing with the wind.

Elk were also found and wild turkey, prairie chicken and quail without number.[16] Overhead in the trees there were little squirrels chattering and leaping from limb to limb. Once in a while a bear would put in his appearance to gaze at the white people and wonder what it was all about. We had foxes and there were bobcats and lynx, both of which were very dangerous when they were cornered. Along the river were the little ring tail raccoons that always go to the trouble of washing their meat before eating.

When night would close down and it was dark beneath the trees and the birds that had sung all day were silent, the moon would shine and the stars would slowly appear. The owls would wake up and the wolves would howl. If our dog would chance to wander far from the cabin, they would chase him and drive him back to the cabin door. He would let out a mournful cry for us to open the door so he could come inside to be safe from the wild dangers that were lurking outside in the darkness.

The fiercest and most dangerous animal with which we had to contend with was the panther. It was a ferocious feline that would turn aside for nothing when aroused. At the back of our cabin along the side of the bluff ran a narrow trail worn deep by the moccasined feet of the Indians and the feet

---

[16] The greater prairie-chicken or pinnated grouse (Tympanuchus cupido), sometimes called a boomer, is a large bird in the grouse family. This North American species was once abundant, but has become extremely rare and extirpated over much of its range due to habitat loss. They are medium to large chicken-like birds, stocky with round-wings. Source: Wikipedia; Greater Prairie Chicken

of the wild things of the wilderness. Early in the night the fierce scream of the panther could be heard coming down this trail.

Their cry sounds so much like the cry of a frightened woman in distress that one feels as though they should go to her assistance, but woe to the man who should be unfortunate enough to make that mistake. We would hear the far-off sound of their cry as they made their way down the trail. It would come nearer and nearer until it would be directly behind our cabin. As the big cat would pass on down the trail, the cry would sound farther and farther away until it would be lost in the distance.

One night a panther came screaming down that trail but he didn't pass on. He stopped and came around in front of our cabin and began sniffing around and beneath the door. To our amazement he soon began climbing to the roof. We could hear the rasping and scratching of his great claws as he ascended the logs. That day Father had shot and dressed a deer and had brought the meat into the cabin. The sneaking, dangerous panther had scented the meat as he came along the trail and was so full of his mean curiosity that he had stopped to investigate. Not being able to gain entrance to the cabin in any other way, he had leaped upon the roof looking for an opening from the top.

We kept the fire burning all night and the hard wood, which was partly covered with ashes, would smoke awhile, then gain strength and flicker and blaze, then smolder down again. No wild animal that ever was created would ever attempt to come down that chimney into the fire, so we knew we were in no danger from that source, but he kept prowling around the cabin until daylight. Father then gave him a bullet from his gun, which he always kept cleaned, loaded and ready for such emergencies.

Not only at night but in the daytime too, we had to be on the lookout for the treacherous panther. He might be lying asleep in the nearest clump of bushes. He might be feigning sleep while lying stretched out upon a limb of some great tree watching for some prey to pass beneath so he could spring down upon its back and with his great claws, rend it to pieces and feast upon its remains.

Our spring was under an overhanging rock beside a small creek that flowed down through the hollow on its way to the river. I carried nearly all the water we used for the household. One day when I was down at the spring, I leaned over and dipped my bucket full of water. When I raised up, I heard to one side of the path in the dark underbrush the sound of bushes rattling and rasping together as though some large creature was passing through them.

I looked around me and just across the little creek stood a huge panther. He was only a few feet from me and when he saw me, he snarled threateningly, lashing his tail on the ground. I tried to reason with myself and to think what would be the best to do. I remembered that Father had often said that God created man the master of the beast and if I should ever come in close contact with them, I must never let them know that I was afraid of them, and never scream or turn my back to them and start running, for if I did, I was sure to be overtaken and torn to pieces.

I realized my will was strong enough to overcome my fear, even though I knew he could kill me, but there was something within me that shrank from facing those cruel, yellow, blood thirsty eyes which leered so wickedly at me.

It is strange how one's mind can be so sensitive and alert to scenes around them when they are facing death or when their lives are hanging in the balance. I was conscious of the whispering of the wind among the leaves. I could hear a Brown Thrush calling and the singing of the little creek that was flowing along over the rocks on its way down to the river while below me a bull frog croaked a hoarse response to my feelings.

All this seemed hours but it must have been only an instant until I gathered up my bucket of water and walking backward several steps, I turned and walked slowly up the hill to the cabin.

Why the great beast didn't spring upon me, I do not know. Perhaps he had recently eaten the best part of a deer and wasn't hungry enough to bother with me, or perhaps he didn't think I was good to eat and I was just trespassing on his territory and he snarled at me to drive me out. When I told Father about the circumstance, he said I had acted very wisely in not screaming or running for if I had done so I would have been torn to pieces immediately.

I believe God can and will take care of His own whether they are in the wild wilderness or in the most protected and peaceful spot on the earth. I had many adventures on that path that led from the cabin to the spring.

One day when I was bringing a bucket of water and had the dog with me, I had just walked under a large limb that projected out over the path when our dog looked upward and growled menacingly. I turned and looked up to where he was gazing and saw a large lynx that was lying out upon the limb basking in the sun. His eyes were half-closed as though he were asleep, but he was really just pretending to be asleep for I could see he was watching the dog. I had passed directly under him and why he didn't spring down upon me and tear me to shreds, I do not know. It was only once that I ever again ventured to go down that path after dark to the spring.

Mother was always very irritable and fretful when she would have anything the matter with her. I believed it was because Father was always so foolish about her and would try so hard to please her and humor her every little whim. One night when she was sick and feverish and the water that I had brought in the evening was warm from long standing in the bucket, she wanted me to get up out of bed and go to the spring and bring her a drink of fresh water.

Father told her that it was cruel and unreasonable to send a child down that path alone in the night and he tried to persuade her to remain alone in the bed until he could go. She refused to let him leave her and still insisted that I go.

I got out of my bed, dressed, took the bucket from the shelf and started down that dark dungeon on my way to the spring. It was very hard to control my fear and walk down that path under the overhanging trees after the experience that I so recently had with a panther. I knew one might be lurking around the spring or climbing among the limbs overhead to spring down upon me at any moment.

Our dear old faithful dog went with me and walked before me going down and behind me coming back to the cabin. I will say again that God will care for His own wherever they chance to be. Whether they are alone in the darkness of the night among the fierce wild beasts of the wilderness or whether they are in a well-protected home in a civilized country, God is everywhere. His power is not limited and I know by my own experience that He will care for His own.

Figure 13: Kee-o-kuk, The Watchful Fox. Thomas Easterly, 1847 daguerreotype, Missouri History Museum. Image enhanced by Ron Ridgway. Image in the public domain.

Born 1780, Illinois Territory. Died June 1848, Kansas.

His cause of death has been attributed to either dysentery, alcoholism or even that he was poisoned by a surviving member of the Black Hawk band. His son Moses succeeded him as chief.

10

Chief Keokuk and the Destroyed Indian Grave

I never liked Chief Keokuk, "the Watchful Fox," as the Indians called him.[17] He was a drunkard and an adulterer, having four wives.[18] Besides, he was so avaricious, nothing mattered to him whether a thing was right or wrong so long as he gained his own desires.

He was born in 1780 and at the time when I first knew him, he was about 57 years of age. He was an eloquent public speaker, but it was disgusting to see a man of his age, even though he be an Indian, always rigged out in bright colors with all the cheap rings and trinkets that could possibly hang on him until he looked like a traveling hardware. Unlike the great Chief Black Hawk, he allowed his braves to drink liquor, which caused them to drift down morally and lose their self-respect until they cared not what they did.

Sometime in the recent past these Indians had buried a squaw in a shallow grave. They had buried her in a sitting position with the top of her head on the level with the ground, then placed logs over the grave and threw a thin layer of dirt over the logs. One afternoon Wash Smith was breaking up a plot of ground on which this grave was located. He had borrowed our oxen and plow and Father had told him about the grave and had warned him not to drive the oxen near it.

"I am not afraid of any gol darn red skin," Wash answered. "Besides there are no Indians near here."

"Wash, if you let those oxen break through into that grave, you will have the devil to pay," Father admonished him. "There are always Indians near and watching the whites. You had better be cautious."

---

[17] Chief Keokuk, a leader of the Sac (Sauk) tribe in central North America, and for decades was one of the most recognized Native American leaders and noted for his accommodation with the U.S. government. Keokuk moved his tribe several times and always acted as an ardent friend of the Americans. His policies were contrary to fellow Sauk leader Black Hawk, who led part of their band to defeat in the Black Hawk War. Source: Wikipedia

[18] Some (unsubstantiated) sources say he may have had up to seven wives.

"Oh, you need not worry about the blasted Indians," Wash answered. "I have shot and scalped more darn red skins than you can count on your fingers and toes. Just let them try any darn thing with me and I'll fill their blasted hides so full of shot they'll look like a gol darn sieve."

Father said no more but he knew that out in that nearby thicket of underbrush there were many dusky forms watching them, and he knew what the result would be if Wash Smith should let those oxen break through into that grave. Soon Wash turned the oxen around again and this time the beasts in turning swayed round directly over the grave. The rotten logs gave way and the oxen stumbled into the grave. In their struggling to get out they trampled the decomposed body until the head was severed from the body and it was crushed down into the bottom of the grave.

The woods had been silent as the grave itself when suddenly the forest echoed from a long, drawn-out quivering yell. It was the war cry of the Indian and immediately Wash Smith was surrounded by a mob of ferocious savages. They yelled and danced around him and waved their glittering tomahawks in a circle above his head.

Father understood the Indian mind as well as the white. He knew the Indians had as much respect and reverence for the graves of their dear loved ones as the white people did. He would not have blamed them if they had killed Wash Smith, but he felt it was his duty to save a life whenever he could.

He sprang between them and Wash, reached out and took hold of their arms and pled desperately for Wash's life. Finally they gave heed to Father's pleading, but they laid hold of Wash and beat and kicked him without mercy, then told him to leave the country.

Father knew Indians for he had wandered through the forest with them, slept in their wigwams and rode beside them in their canoes until he knew all their signs and customs. He knew this deal was not ended here but there would be more trouble with them now. He knew they would wait until Wash went back to his cabin and then they would massacre him and burn his cabin to the ground. He felt he must protect Wash if he could, so he brought him and our oxen home to our cabin.

Wash Smith was the kind of a man who could be very brave when trouble and danger was far away in the distance, but when it came near, he was very cowardly as he was when he had first come here and was staying at our cabin. One night a panther screamed somewhere out in the woods and Wash began mocking it. When the panther would scream, Wash would scream answering it. Now this was very amusing while the laugh was all on the panther, but suddenly the panther screamed out very near Wash's side. He was so badly frightened he jumped into the cabin, slammed the heavy door shut and slid the bar into its place. As if that wasn't enough to keep the panther from coming inside, he rolled our flour barrel against the door, and so it was now with the Indians.

While there was no trouble, he could brag about the great number of red skins he had shot and scalped but now after getting the Indians enraged and on the warpath, he was almost like a helpless child looking to my father for his protection. All night long he kept listening and gazing around into the dark corners of the cabin as though there might be the dark forms of Indians lurking there, ready to spring out upon him at any moment if a sudden gust of wind swept through the woods or if a twig loosened and dropped down on the roof of the cabin.

"What was that noise, John?" he would ask, with a certain expression of fright and despair in his voice, and his anxiety seemed to increase as the night wore on. Although I had never been afraid of anything in my life, I had to admit to myself, there was a weird menace lurking around out in that night. The hair on our dog's neck stood straight up all night long and he would growl menacingly down deep in his throat from time to time. Even our oxen, as dumb as they were, grew uneasy and trampled around in their stalls and sometimes they would bellow aloud with fright. I knew without being told that our little clearing was surrounded by painted warriors.

Next morning just after we had finished eating our breakfast, Father gazed out of the window and saw a young Indian brave coming into our clearing. He was one whom Father had befriended on several occasions. It is true an Indian never forgets or forgives a wrong, but neither does he forget a kindness.

Father knew the moment he saw him coming that there was something in the wind by the way the Indian was walking and acting. He came into our cabin and stood like a stone statue against the wall. Father waited with patience for him to speak but he did not speak until Father told Wash Smith to leave the cabin and stay quietly in the stable while the Indian remained. Sometime after Wash left the cabin the Indian spoke.

"A true warrior never lies to his friend," he said. He relapsed into silence again and again, Father waited. After another long interval, he spoke again: "When young braves paint their faces and dance like Keokuk's braves did last night, they are on the warpath. There will be wailing and bloodshed in the white man's cabin tonight," he said, and then he was gone, disappearing as silently as if he had been only a phantom. The trees and underbrush gave back no more sound than if he had not passed through them.

I never realized until that morning what a wonderful man my father was. He was well educated and he was a perfect gentleman in every sense of the word. Since we had come out here to the Iowa Territory, I had been his constant companion. I had played near him while he cut down trees and made them into rails for our fencing. I had dropped seeds into the ground while he covered them with his hoe. I rode on the river with him, sitting beside him in his boat. He was my teacher, not only in my books, but he taught me to understand the secrets of the wilderness until it held no terror for me. He instructed me how to be indifferent to the howling of the wolf pack and to ignore the ferocious scream of the panther when it would be pouncing upon its prey.

He taught me the names and nature of the different trees and how to find my way out if I became lost in the woods. He taught me how to strip the slippery elm of its bark and how to gather the different herbs and dig black root. Quite often we would drift back into the thickest gloom of the woods where the moisture from the last year's rotten leaves would ooze out beneath our moccasined feet and gather leaves and roots that had too long and hard names for a child of my age to remember, but I knew them. I knew what they were for and how to boil them down and prepare them into medicine for the family use. He was my hero and I loved him more than I loved anyone else in the world.

That morning, I looked at my father and thought how handsome he was. I can see him yet as he stood there fearless and at ease even at a time like this when it seemed as though our very lives were hanging in the balance. Father had never met anything he was afraid of and it was likely that to his dying day he never would but he never bragged.

He would remain quiet and reason a thing out, and make up his mind what was the best thing to do for those who were depending upon him. I contrasted him to Wash Smith, who was then crouching in the corner of the cabin with his hair and whiskers all tousled and his head fallen forward upon his knees in a dejected attitude. As I watched him, I had a crazy impulse to laugh and I did laugh.

"I wish I could know whether old Keokuk will be drunk tonight or not," Father said. "If he isn't drunk, he will control his braves, for he knows well what the soldiers at Ft. Armstrong will do to him and his tribe if they should do harm to a white settler, but if he is lying around some place dead drunk as he usually is, his warriors will take advantage of that and no cabin in this neighborhood will be safe. I believe it is best for us to go."

When he said this, he began loading our things into our wagon while Wash Smith brought the oxen around. We drove to the Casteel cabin and told them of the trouble and they soon had their horses loaded with their household equipment and we started south toward Keokuk, Iowa, where there was already a small settlement of white people. Our little cabin was left abandoned and alone in the vast wilderness.[19] [20]

---

[19] The story of the disturbed grave is assumed to be true, and may well have infuriated the Indians, but there were other issues at play. The Indians' annuity had not been paid and they were in the midst of a land boundary dispute. When they were unable to get redress after sending a delegation to Washington, D.C., their anger spilled upon the white settlers.

[20] A man named Thomas Baker had settled very near the Indian settlement and the Indians were unhappy with his livestock being so near them. In April 1837, Chief Wapello went to the cabin

Figure 14: Fox and Sac War Dance. Charles Joseph Hullmandel, printer and Peter Rindisbacher, 1839. Library of Congress. Image in the public domain.

Figure 15: Chief Wapello; Wa-Pel-La The Prince, A Musquakee Chief, painted by Charles Bird King. Lithographed, colored and published ca 1836-1844 by J.T. Bowen, Philadelphia. Image in the public domain.

of Richard Moore to tell him the tribe wanted Mr. Baker to go, but that Mr. Moore would not be disturbed. The next day Baker was driven from his claim and his cabin burned. About a week later, a number of Indians appeared at Richard Moore's cabin and told him he must also go. He gathered his family and he and Mary Ann's family left for Henry County. Source: Portrait & Biographical Album of Washington County, Iowa, 1887. Note: Henry County was one of the original subdivisions of Des Moines County, where Keokuk is located. Both families returned in 1839.

11.

Murder in Keokuk, Iowa

In June 1820 there stood one lone cabin at the foot of Puckeshetuck, or the foot of the rapids, which is now called Keokuk.[21] It was built by Dr. Samuel Muir who was a surgeon in the U.S. Army located at Ft. Edwards, now Warsaw, Illinois.

At the head of the rapids was an Indian village. Their chief was Wapello, or "Cut Nose," and below the creek, running into the river on the lower side of the Indian town, were the remains of a deserted trading house around which was growing a number of apple trees.[22]

People who had met Dr. Samuel Muir described him as a man of medium height, light complexioned, pale blue eyes, temperate in his habits and precise in his business dealings. Dr. Muir married a Sac Indian girl who dreamed of a white man who was her husband and when she met Dr. Muir, she knew he was the man of her dreams. After they were married and had one child, he deserted her and went back to the Army but taking their child in a boat, she rowed down the river to where Dr. Muir was located.[23]

When he realized what great love she had for him, he withdrew from the army and went back with her to the foot of the rapids and lived there with her until the Asiatic Cholera broke out among the army. He then went back to do what he could for the soldiers, but he took the cholera himself and died on September 24, 1832. Dr. Muir and his Indian wife had four children. They were: Louisa, James, Mary and Sophia. When Dr. Muir died, his wife and their youngest children drifted away with her Indian tribe and were never heard

---

[21] Indian name for Keokuk.

[22] Wapello was born in 1787 at Prairie du Chien, Northwest Territory. Short and stout in physical stature, with a kindly visage, Wapello entertained friendly relations with white settlers throughout his life. During the Black Hawk War, he supported Chief Keokuk. Source: Wikipedia

[23] In 1820, the U.S. Army prohibited soldiers stationed along the Mississippi River from having wives who were Native American. Dr. Muir resigned his commission rather than leave his Indian wife and crossed the river to resettle. He built a log cabin for them at the bottom of the bluff near Main and Water Streets, and became the area's first white settler. Source: Wikipedia

from again. Louisa Muir, their oldest daughter, married a white man and remained in Keokuk. I have often seen her and remember her well.

In the spring of 1828, Moses Stillwell with his wife and four children and a man by the name of Van Ansdal came and settled at the foot of the rapids and lived there until his death about 1834. Stillwell cut wood and sold to steamboats, which occasionally passed up the river selling knives, calico cloth and blankets to the Indians.

There was the Dedman family who came in 1828 but went away again in 1830.

Dr. Isaac Galland came next in 1829.[24] His daughter Elenor was the first white female child born in Lee County.

In 1830 Isaac R. Campbell and his family moved over from Nauvoo, or Commerce as it was then called, and settled at the foot of the falls.[25] Samuel Brierly, the father of James Brierly, who was the first legislator representative from Lee County, came the same year.[26] These people whom I have mentioned were all respectable citizens.

When the roads settled in the spring of 1835, or the ground settled, for there were not many roads - just trails through the woods and across the prairies - numerous home-seekers and claim-hunters began to come in. Sometimes the head of a family came first and selected a location and then went back and brought his family. In other cases, the entire family came at one time. Sometimes coming all the way from the old home in Ohio, Indiana, Kentucky, Virginia, New York and Pennsylvania in wagons and sometimes by boat down the Ohio River and up the Mississippi River.

---

[24] Dr. Galland established the settlement of Nashville on the west bank of the Mississippi River in what is now Lee County, Iowa, where he practiced medicine and founded a trading post. He promoted Nashville as a future commercial center and when families joined the settlement, Galland hired a teacher and built a log house founding the first school in what would become Iowa Territory. In the harsh frontier conditions, his wife died, leaving him with two very young children. Source: Wikipedia

[25] Kept the first tavern in Keokuk. Source: *History of Lee County, A.T. Andreas Illustrated Historical Atlas of the State of Iowa*, 1875, transcribed by Sara Hemp.

[26] Elected to the House of Representatives of the first Legislative Assembly of the Iowa Territory in 1838, representing Lee County. Source: The Iowa Legislature

Until the year of 1837 the city had no name. It was called by some, "Puckeshetuck," others called it "The Point," while there were others who called it "The Rapids." Dr. Galland laid out the town plat and it was named in honor of the great Chief Keokuk. The first sale of town lots was in June 1837. That sure was a great day; even a large steamboat came up the Mississippi River from St. Louis loaded down with passengers to attend the sale.

In 1838 when we came to Keokuk it had a population of about 150 people.[27] Then one L.B. Fleak came and bought the Dr. Muir house and beside this he put up a building in which he ran a hotel.[28] I can well remember the Dr. Muir house. It was a double log cabin with a kitchen built in the back and there was a root cellar which nowadays we call a "vegetable cave" and too, there was a log stable with a large garden.

In the early pioneer days, the Mississippi River was a great highway and the little village of Keokuk was a waterfront town; quite often a few criminals would float in and remain for a time, then go to their headquarters at Bellevue. There were gangs of horse thieves, murderers, gamblers, men who passed counterfeit money and all other kinds of cut throats who had committed crimes in the eastern states.[29] When the law got too hot on their trail, they would flee west to the little frontier towns on the Mississippi River.

There were wood choppers who would drift in a few at a time. The majority of these were single men, although there were a few who had families. These wood choppers were rough, rugged ex-soldiers who had fought at the

---

[27] Even in July 1841, the population was estimated at 150. By 1846, it had risen to 500. Source: City of Keokuk official website.

[28] The first duly-authorized Postmaster, appointed June 24, 1841. Source: City of Keokuk official website.

[29] An excerpt from an article by Francis J. Helenthal, originally printed in the *Shoppers Free Press,* December 4,1974. "Some of the best accounts of early Keokuk in the first half of the ninetieth century were recorded by those who came to Nauvoo with the first Saints in 1839 and during the building of that boomtown into the 40s. One such description reads: 'The river bottoms, and the Half Breed Tract just across the Mississippi in Iowa, were notoriously infested with horse thieves, counterfeiters, cut-throats, and brigands. Some of the outlaw gangs had become so powerful as to be politically potent." According to the article, Robert B. Ogden wrote of his experiences on his way to Keokuk. Before arriving, he chanced upon a woman who pleaded with him in tears to not go to Keokuk. She was quoted as saying, "It's the wickedest place in the United States... Nothing but thieves and gamblers and every night somebody's robbed... and the number of people killed is awful."

famous Battle of Bad Axe where they slaughtered the great Chief Black Hawk's army of braves. There were hunters, fur traders, raft men and farmers who swelled the population of Keokuk at various times.

After we were well settled in our new home in the village of Keokuk, Father contracted with a steamboat company to furnish wood for their engines, and among the choppers he hired was a man who called himself "Smith" for the time being. There were several Smiths, Jones and Browns among them - too many. This man Smith was a large, burly man. He always carried a dark, malignant scowl on his visage and was a leader of a slick horse thief gang, but even a horse thief gets short of money at times and must earn a little by working until he can steal a horse or two and get them turned into cash.

Father put them to work on the hillside at the back of our cabin. The trees they were chopping were big heavy timber which perhaps had taken a hundred years or more to grow. Among the choppers was a man who called himself Brown and it seemed as though Brown was never known to buy tobacco, but always chewed at the expense of others.

This afternoon the party had been drinking quite heavily and the horse thief Smith was the kind of man who was high-tempered and ugly when drinking. Brown kept insisting Smith give him a chew of tobacco and Smith, who was getting more and more restless and angry as the afternoon wore on, told him to buy his own tobacco. He exclaimed with a violent oath that if Brown asked him again for tobacco, he would cut his throat for him. The contention kept brewing until Smith, in a terrible rage, drew a sharp dagger from his belt and made a dive at Brown's neck. Father, who was sitting on a log directing the choppers, sprang forward.

"You, Smith, put up that knife!" he shouted. "You crazy fool, you!" he exclaimed as he seized the burly horse thief and whirled him around out of reach of Brown, and reaching for Brown, thrust him aside roughly.

"You fellows behave yourselves or get out," he said, but when he turned to go back to the log again, Smith drew his knife, and sweeping it through the air, struck Brown in the neck and severed his jugular vein. Brown fell down on the ground beside a log and died. His life ebbing out stained the leaves with his blood.

Mother, Emily and I ran to the window and looked out when we heard the loud, hoarse shouts of the men. I could scarcely believe what I saw, for it seemed to me that it was beyond reason that on such a beautiful autumn day that a dark tragedy like murder could take place. While we watched from the window, suddenly we heard a wild, hysterical scream and a woman came running from some cabin farther south of ours and threw herself down upon the ground beside the body of the dying man. Her body writhed as though in convulsions and the cry which came from her lips sounded sometimes like a prayer and then it would sound as though it had turned to a curse. The way she carried on made me think of the wind - how I had seen it blow from some dark cloud - how it writhes, twists and bends the bushes almost to the ground, but helps no one, nor does it do anything any good.

"Mother, why does the woman scream, carry on and act like that for?" Emily asked.

"Well, I suppose the murdered man must be her husband and perhaps she loved him, and now that he has been cruelly murdered, she has lost control of herself and given over to this intense grief," she answered.

Soon an ox cart came rumbling along the dusty road filled with men to pick up the body.

When this horrible thing occurred, the choppers quit work and scattered about town. The burly horse thief Smith disappeared into the woods. No one offered to pursue him. I suppose the citizens of Keokuk thought that one more or less horse thief around didn't matter very much. Perhaps when he emerged from the woods and appeared among civilized people again his name would not be Smith but would be Jones or Brown.

That was the first murder I had ever witnessed and it made everything seem strange to me. The river sounded louder than usual, not music, but moaning. Out in the woods even the stumps took on huge, surprising shapes and seemed to come alive and move around from time to time. That night the logs upon the hearth flamed and purred and sent out their cheerful light just as they always did. It was the same room with its same walls of logs, beams and rafters and the same puncheon floor, but the wind shrieking down the chimney did not sing as usual - instead it screamed, wailed and sobbed and cried. To me, it was mocking the voice of that hysterical woman in her sorrow and distress.

I tried to read aloud from the Bible but I made so many mistakes Father became disgusted and took the book from me and finished reading the chapter. He then sent me off to bed.

All through the autumn days that woman would come there, sit upon that log and moan and cry over that blood stain on the leaves until the winter snow came and covered it all from her sight.

Figure 16: The Levee at Keokuk, Foot of High Street, 1848.
Image in the public domain.

12

The Skinny-Dipper & The Coin Thief

I didn't like living in Keokuk, for I was not allowed to go out of our own yard even to the river or to walk along the old Indian trail, which ran along the side of the bluff back of our cabin, unless Father was with me. I had to stay in our own yard all day. Father said there were too many rough men straggling around through the woods.

"What difference does that make?" I asked. "There were men scattered all through the woods around our cabin where we lived before we came here to Keokuk and you let me go as I pleased while living there," I protested.

"Mary Ann, those men were Indians and they were the kind of men who would never harm a little girl like you," he answered. "These men who roam the woods around here are a very different class of men from the Indians. There is nothing too bad or too low for them to do."

Father put up a swing in a tree near our door and helped us to build a play house under the tree. He commanded sister Emily and me to stay there and never go beyond the limits of our yard. Mother taught me to sew and do housework and I soon found that it was really more fun to do real cooking than to just play at it by making mud pies. It wasn't very long until I could get the dinner alone with her sitting near in a chair directing me.

The summer of 1839 slipped away and autumn came. Out in the woods there were wild grape vines hanging from the trees loaded down with purple grapes. The ripe nuts were falling and through the forest and over the woods and river there hung a blue haze, soft and dreamy. The little yellow birds that had not yet gone south flitted about among the hazel bushes. Yellow hammers pounded on the hardwood of the dead trees while crows and hawks circled around overhead. I would want to go into the woods and be a part of these things. Emily was older now and had more will of her own and she too demanded more freedom and refused to stay inside so much.

One beautiful autumn day Father took us girls to the river to fish. We were sitting upon the bank fishing when we heard a stamping in the bushes and a horse appeared. He was running loose with a saddle on his back and his halter rope dragging. Suddenly there was a darker shadow in the water and looking across the river I saw the largest and fleshiest woman I had ever seen before, nor have I ever seen one so large and fleshy since.

She had abruptly emerged from the underbrush and hastily removing all her clothing, she plunged into the river and swam across to within a few feet of where we were sitting. She paid no attention to us but ran as fast as she could after the horse. I had never seen such a strange sight in all my life. She was entirely in the nude with the brilliant morning sun shining full upon her figure. Her hair was tumbling in wet curls and ringlets over her fat, heavy shoulders. She caught the horse, then after tying him to a limb of a tree, she plunged into the river again and swam across to the opposite bank, where she put on her clothes and disappeared from sight.

I was so amazed I could not utter a word and for a long time I could not even think coherently. I looked around at Father and he was laughing until he could hardly sit up. As we walked up to the house carrying the fish we had caught, he said, "We will not say anything about this instance to anyone, girls. No, not even to your mother, for it is too ridiculous and indecent to even talk about." I told him I would not say anything about it to any one and I never did, until now as I am telling you.

While mother was alone in the cabin that morning, she lay down upon the bed to rest and soon fell asleep. Suddenly, she was awakened by the soft closing of the door. She roused herself to a sitting position and felt a dull numbness stealing over her, but she slid from the bed to the floor and stole silently across the room to the door. When she opened it and looked out, she caught a glimpse of a man's back as he was disappearing into the underbrush at the back of our cabin. She was so frightened she did not know what to do. She then remembered that Father had some gold coins laid away. He had saved them to purchase some cows and a team of horses to take back with us when the way opened, so we could go back to our land, which we had left when the Indians had driven the white people out of that country.

She arose from her chair and went to the place where the gold coins were put away and found to her dismay that they were gone. When Father and we girls returned home she was so nervous and upset she was almost in hysteria, but she described the man's back the best she could in the nervous condition she was in. Father was a psychologist and a seer as well. He could read men and knew well what they were capable of doing and he had quite an idea who the man was who had stolen his gold coins.

That evening Father walked over to a neighbor's house to visit for a while, as was the custom in those early days in Iowa Territory. During their conversation, Father related how some thief had entered his home and robbed him of his gold coins. Beside the fireplace there stood a gallon jug made from crockery and as the man discussed the story of the thief, he kept looking around at the jug. Father was able to read his glances and knew the workings of his mind, for he had been watching him very closely as he talked.

Suddenly Father rose from the chair on which he was sitting, walked over to the fireplace and, reaching out, he took up the tongs that were lying near and gave the jug a whack with them. It broke into small pieces and among the shattered pieces of the jug lay Father's gold coins. He reached down, gathered them up and walked out the door. Nothing was ever said about the affair, but that man always afterward remained very shy when my father was any place around.

13.

The Woods Colt Baby and the Panther

Although Keokuk was getting thickly settled, there were still many large wild animals roving around in the woods. We would often hear the mournful howls of the ravenous wolf pack and the wild screams of the panther. Sometimes at night we could even hear the big cats scratching on the rail fence that enclosed a plat of ground around our log stable. Occasionally someone would have a narrow escape from being torn to pieces by these wild beasts.

In Keokuk in the fall of 1838, two women, a woods colt baby and a dog were walking along a path that had been an old Indian trail.[30] Suddenly they heard a rustling in the underbrush. As they watched, a large Yellow Timber Lynx stepped out of the brush into the path in front of them.

When the lynx saw them, he climbed up into a tree, and crawling out upon a limb, he sat snarling down at them. They were afraid to walk under the tree, for they knew the vicious beast would spring down upon their backs as they made their way along the path.

They stopped walking and while they were taking counsel together about what was the best and safest thing to do, the lynx became impatient and came down the tree and attacked the dog. These women, however, were not the timid kind, for they were true pioneers. They were not so easily frightened as the women of these civilized times who scream with fright when they see an innocent, helpless little mouse.

While one of them held the woods colt baby, the other gathered a large heavy club and watching her chance, struck the lynx a violent blow, which broke his back, paralyzing him and making him helpless. She and the dog finished him and the two women, the woods colt baby, and the dog went on their way down the path.

---

[30] Wood Colts Baby: A child born out of wedlock.

14

Courting By Moonlight

In those early pioneer days, the pith from a cow's horn made into tea was a sure cure for convulsions. One night when one of our neighbor women was very sick and having convulsions, someone present spoke of the cow's horn remedy. It was then the sick lady's husband remembered when he was hoeing in his garden, he had found a cow's horn and after picking it up he had stuck it into the fork of a tree just beyond the garden.

Two young women who were there offered to go and get it for them. They went out into the night and made their way to the tree and reaching up, they had just grasped the cow's horn when a panther gave a loud fierce scream somewhere in the dark woods just beyond the garden. The girls, still clinging to the cow's horn, turned and fled toward the house with the treacherous feline pursuing them.

When they reached the house and sprang inside, as they slammed the door shut and dropped the bar into its place, the panther came leaping with all his strength against the door but the heavy door did not give way. When he realized his prey had made its escape, he set up a tremendous cry of rage and disappointment.

In those early days of Iowa Territory, the young people courted principally by moonlight, that is if there was a moon, and if not done by moonlight, it was done in the cabin with the lights out and the embers covered with ashes. That was a good way too, for the old folks would be sleeping in the same room.

Those were the days when people went pleasure riding with an ox team and wagon, or sometimes they had an ox cart.

I can well remember the night when Zeak went a courting. Zeak was tall, dark and handsome, and I might add, brilliant. He could go with any girl in Keokuk or anywhere round about, for no girl in her right mind could resist the mystery of Zeak's flashing bright eyes. Whenever he came near a girl, she would start dreaming of wedding bells, although it was only the sound of old brindle's cow bell coming from the nearby woods that she was listening to.

This night of which I speak, Zeak went calling on Betsey who lived in the last house out down the river road. Well, they called it a road but it was just a sort of a stump-lined alley – anyway, it led down the river to a one-room log cabin where Betsey lived. Betsey wasn't a very pretty girl, for she had straw-colored hair and freckles on her nose, but she possessed that ineffable, impalpable something which is like the wind, no one could tell whence it cometh or whether it goeth, but Betsey had it. That made her a rare, precious thing among the Keokuk boys. Zeak was one of the few boys she would go out with. That night Zeak stayed with Betsey until the fire had burned low and the logs lay reduced to a dull heap of embers and there was only a tiny spark left on the tallow dip.

What is a tallow dip, did you ask?[31] Well, to make a tallow dip, take a receptacle that will hold melted lard or tallow and small enough to be carried conveniently and of a noncombustible nature (the pioneers used a common saucer). Fill it about half full of melted tallow or lard, then get an old piece of soft cotton cloth and tear off a strip an inch or so wide and about a foot long. Twist it and then take hold of the ends and let it untwist into a loose rope. Place the doubled end into the grease and let the loose ends extend slightly over the rim of the saucer and apply the match to the end that is hanging over, that is - if you have a match. The pioneers didn't have matches; they lit their tallow dips with a coal from the fireplace.

Zeak kissed Betsey goodnight and got on his horse and started home. The way home was both dark and treacherous. The road was lined on both sides by tall oak, walnut and hickory trees. One great tree had blown over by the wind and the top had lodged in the tops of the trees on the opposite side

---

[31] Tallow once was widely used to make molded candles before more convenient wax varieties became available and for some time after since they continued to be a cheaper alternative. For those unable to avail themselves of homemade, molded tallow candles, the "tallow dip"—a reed that had been dipped in melted tallow or sometimes a strip of burning cloth in a saucer of tallow grease—was an accessible substitute.

of the road and as Zeak rode under it, a vicious panther that was lying out upon the trunk of the huge tree, which extended across the road, sprang down and landed upon the horse just back of Zeak's saddle.

All that saved Zeak was the heavy bulk of the panther. His great claws stuck deep into the horse's hips but the weight of the panther was too great for the tender flesh of the horse. He slid backward, his long sharp claws tearing a wide slash on either side of the animal clear to the bone. The wounded horse gave a wild, pathetic scream of terror and agony and ran, but Zeak was a good rider and remained in the saddle and held on with all his might. The horse did not stop running until it reached home to his own stable. I saw the horse the next day with the great gashes lying open on either hip, which were still bleeding profusely.

Figure 17: Soap making. Image in the public domain.

15.

The Witch

In the early pioneer days people made their own soap. They would bore holes in the bottom of a barrel and then set it upon a broad board that was propped up a foot or so above the ground and on a slant. They then placed straw in the bottom of the barrel and dumped in hickory ashes on top of the straw. They always used hickory ashes because they contain the proper amount of potassium carbonate to form the alkaline solution when extracted by water.

A bucket of water was then poured over the ashes. They placed the straw in the barrel as a strainer for the lye as it seeps through the hickory ashes. They hallowed the ashes at the top and pressed it against the sides of the barrel all around so the water would seep through the center and not run down the sides of the barrel, but would drip from the lower side into an iron kettle or a jar made of crockery that is set beneath to catch it.

When the kettle was full it was tested by dropping an egg into it. If the egg floated the lye was strong enough to be put in the large kettle for heating to the proper degree for the reception of grease scraps and meat rind, which the housewife had been collecting and saving for many months for that purpose.

After boiling a sufficient length of time, the lye and grease unite, producing a soft soap suitable for general family use or it may be hardened by adding the proper amount of salt, then cut into bars of any desirable shape or size.

One day our neighbor woman had a barrel arranged and was running off lye to make soap when a cow that was running at large in the village of Keokuk came along and, sticking her nose into the kettle of lye, drank freely of it. Immediately the cow became frantic and after running and snorting for a time as if she had been bitten by a mad dog and had taken the rabies, she fell down dead. There was no dog in Keokuk that had gone made with rabies, so the man who owned the cow believed she had been bewitched and a friend told him if he would cover the dead cow with straw and trash and set fire to her, the witch would come to him while she was burning.

Several days before this, the owner of the cow had borrowed one of Father's saws. He was the kind of man who never was known to return the articles he would borrow of others. Father needed his saw and went there to get it while the cow was burning. The owner of the cow was sullen and at first refused to speak, then suddenly he turned on Father, and in a very angry tone of voice accused him of bewitching his cow. Father knew the cow had drank lye but he was so disgusted at such ignorance and folly that he did not try to explain to the man that he was not a witch and had no power to bewitch anything. He walked over to the cabin door where his saw was lying on the ground, picked it up and came back home. I suppose the foolish fellow ever afterward believed my father was a witch and had bewitched his only cow.

There was a woman living in Keokuk who wanted to be a witch. She made her clothes look as slouchy as possible. Oft times going around with an old shoe on one of her feet and perhaps a man's old worn-out boot on the other. She would walk bent forward leaning on a crooked hickory stick striving to make herself appear as hideous as possible. She was in the habit of walking into the neighbor's homes and taking whatever she wanted. The housewife was afraid of her sorcery and would not contrary her whatever she did. Her cynical glance and sullen, weird smile were those of a hag, which indeed would lead a superstitious woman to believe her a witch. There was also something about her makeup to justify the aversion and fear which people felt when they would see her approaching their home.

One afternoon she came to our house and saw some yarn she wanted, but as she reached to take it, Mother, who was not afraid of her sorcery, succeeded in getting a hold on the yarn first. Placing it in a chair, she sat down upon it. The old hag flew into a violent rage and began to threaten Mother with her enchantment. She waved her arms above her head and called down the power of darkness to her assistance.

"I would have you know that I am not afraid of your witchcraft, neither am I afraid of your power of darkness." Mother exclaimed.

When she saw Mother wasn't afraid of her witchcraft, she changed her tactics and began to accuse her of infidelity to her husband.

"You have deceived your husband, and that is a great crime. Oh, I know what kind of woman you are, for I can read your past as well as your present. And too, you have broken up another home." She raved on, "You have robbed a man of his joy. When your husband hears of all this what will he do? Oh, I know what he will do. He will not forgive you this, but he will drive you from his home. Now give me the yarn, or I will tell him of your deceit and shame."

Mother was a very neat housekeeper. She always kept her kitchen utensils scoured and washed clean and turned upside down on a pot bench that stood beside the fireplace.

When the old hag saw she could not frighten Mother any other way, she walked over to the pot bench and, turning all the kitchen utensils right side up, she wet her finger with saliva from her mouth and made crosses in the bottom of each one. Turning to Mother she exclaimed:

"You'll be sorry for this. Soon disaster will come to your home, your husband shall hear of your indecent conduct and he will turn you out like the miserable wretch which indeed you are." With a vicious, malicious smile toward Mother, she made her way out of the cabin.

Young as I was, I thought of how absurd that line of talk was. My dear mother, who was almost an invalid and how Father loved her with such a deep self-sacrificing devotion. I know if the old hag went to him with her line of talk just about what kind of treatment she would get, but she did not go near him. In fact, she never went near my father about anything, for she stood in too much fear of him. She would not even look at him for she was afraid of those deep-seeing eyes that she knew could read her very soul and she always shrank back from him if she chanced to meet him when unaware of his passing.

Figure 18: Chief Black Hawk, the Sac war chief and namesake of the Black Hawk War of 1832. George Catlin, Smithsonian American Art Museum. Image in the public domain.

Figure 19: Governor Robert Lucas portrait by John Henry Witt. First Governor of Iowa Territory (1838-1841). He was also the 12th Governor of Ohio. Image in the public domain.

16

Going Back to Our Little Cabin in the Woods

Two years had now passed since we had come to Keokuk and great things had taken place during those two years of 1838 and '39. The great Chief Black Hawk had died and had been buried with full honors in what is now called Davis County on the bank of the Des Moines River. Dr. James Turner had stolen the skull with the idea of exhibiting it in the east for profit.[32]

It being the skull of the great famous Chief Black Hawk, who was known throughout the whole country at that time, Dr. Turner might have become rich if his plans had materialized - but they didn't. He was pursued from place to place until he became desperate and gave the skull to a doctor at Quincy, Illinois. Dr. Turner was never captured but he fled from place to place to evade capture until at last he got his punishment by dying with the cholera.

President Van Buren, having great confidence and trusting the abilities and integrity of Robert Lucas, appointed him governor of the Iowa territory.[33]

Lucas went to Iowa City with his two daughters and took General Flutcher as guide.[34] They rode on horseback to the new capitol where they were entertained at the most fancy, up-to-date house in the city. When night came on the new governor and his two daughters climbed to the attic on a ladder and went to bed. It was the only house in Iowa City at that time that could boast of having an attic.

The settlers in and around Iowa City were mostly young men who had no families. They were lone men who made their way through the woods on

---

[32] Dr. Turner severed the head from the body and then cooked the flesh off of the skull. When the Indians came looking for Dr Turner, he hid and finally made his escape with his wife in a canoe. After giving it to the doctor in Quincy, IL for safekeeping, the doctor refused to return it. Source: Story by Mrs. Sarah Welch Nossaman published in *Annals of Iowa*, October 1922.

[33] The 12th governor of Ohio, serving from 1832 to 1836. He also served as the first governor of the Iowa Territory from 1838 to 1841.

[34] Third and last territorial capital of Iowa.

foot bringing with them a gun, a knife, a bake pan and a tin cup. Their food while traveling to the new country consisted of a small sack of corn meal and a small slab of bacon. When they arrived, they built themselves log cabins to live in and any traveler who might chance to pass that way was welcome to come in and pass the night with them. Even whenever these men would go hunting or go away from their cabins on any errand, he would leave his door unfastened so someone passing through the country could enter and make himself at home.

Yes, Iowa City was the capitol of the new Iowa Territory but where was Iowa City? It was a small cluster of log cabins that were nestled in the brush on the Iowa River - but where? There was hardly anyone who was able to find it. So, the settlers employed Lyman Dillon to run a furrow of plowed ground across the prairie and through the woods to guide strangers to the new capitol and seat of government, for there was no road leading into the town.

Dillon started from Dubuque with his huge breaking plow drawn by five yoke of oxen. He took with him an emigrant wagon to haul his cooking utensils and provisions and other necessities for the long hard journey. Day after day he plowed, turning over the tough prairie sod, mile after mile to mark the way for both citizens and strangers to reach the new capitol. At noon and night, the oxen were turned loose to graze on the rich prairie grass while Dillon and his helpers cooked their food and slept in the wagon. When they reached Iowa City, they had plowed a furrow nearly one hundred miles long. I know of no other furrow that was ever plowed that many miles long.

Iowa Territory had a newspaper - "The Dubuque Visitor" - that had been established at the Dubuque lead mines in 1836 by John King. William Cary Jones from Chillicothe, Ohio had charge of the mechanical department of the office. The foreman and chief typesetter was a man from Galena, Illinois by the name of Andrew Keesecker. James Clark edited a newspaper at Flint Hills. It was called "The Iowa Territorial Gazette."

Settlers were pouring into what is now Lee County in streams. In Keokuk we could hear nothing but the ringing of the axes as the white emigrants chopped the trees down and at night the whole country would be lighted up by the fires from the burning brush heaps they had cleared from the land through the day.

Huge oaks with their great spreading branches, no one knew how many years they had been in reaching such majestic height, were brought down with such loud crashes they would shake the very ground we were standing on and rattle the sash and glass in our cabin window. The white men shot off the deer for sport just to be able to brag about the great number they could kill in a day. They tore up the country until one who hadn't seen it for two years would never recognize it as the same place.

To me, everything seemed so cluttered up and dirty. There were times when I even imagined the whole country round about smelled bad. I longed to go back home to the fresh, clean forest where the Indians lived.

One day Father came in from his work and placing a chair near to where Mother was sitting, he sat down and reached over, taking her soft, white hand. My mother's hands were too soft and too white for a pioneer woman.

"Sally," he began, "now we can go back to our own land in the wilderness if we choose. I know you weren't born for the wilderness and I know how hard a road it is for you to travel. Honey, if you would rather go back to Indiana, to live where it will be more comfortable and easy for you, I will take you back."

There was a tired weariness in her voice when she answered him. "No," she said. "I know the pioneer road is indeed a hard road to travel, but we chose it, and now we will not go back. We will go on."

"Then you will go willingly with me?" he asked, looking pleadingly into her face.

"I will go with you anywhere, John," she answered unfaltering.

I was very glad to hear them make up their minds as they did, for I didn't want to go back to Indiana. I was homesick for our little log cabin in the wilderness and although I never would have admitted it then, I was homesick for the Indians and the wild, free life they lived.

When my father made up his mind to do a thing, he just went ahead and did it, and that was all there was to it. Now he had his mind made up to go back to his own land and it wasn't long until we were on our way.

We were quite a caravan. Father had bought a nice team of horses and some cows. We already had a pet sheep and our dear old dog that we had brought with us from Indiana. Mother was bringing along ten hens and a rooster and Emily had a pet kitten.

Father drove the horses that were hitched to the wagon while Wash Smith, who was going along back with us, drove the cattle behind the wagon. It wasn't very long until the cattle learned to follow and there wasn't very much driving to do. We were on our way home to the dearest and happiest home that I have ever known.

Figure 20: Vintage covered wagon near log house in grass

17

Home Sweet Home

As we drove along, we saw the ash heaps where the cabins that had been built by the white men had all been burned down by the Indians. There weren't many ash heaps, for there were only a few white settlers in that region anywhere about, but the cabins, log stables and rail fences were all gone. Think what joy we felt when we came in sight of our own clearing and saw on the hillside above the beautiful Iowa River our own little log cabin standing in the shadow of the gnarled old oak and hickory trees just as we had left it.

As I look back through the long years that have passed since then, I can see the place as plain as if it were only yesterday. The little log cabin, the log stable with the rail fence surrounding it and the lodges and wigwams of the Sac and Fox Indians clustered together in the vale below. I have no words to make you understand just how beautiful the scene was. In fact, there is no one but a poet who could describe the place and do it justice.

When Father drove up into the clearing, I leaped from the wagon and ran to the door of the cabin. It was not barred and when I opened it the long unused wooden hinges squeaked and groaned. I stepped inside and gazed about me. Nothing had been changed. It was just as we had left it.

The fire was dead and the ashes were scattered upon the hearth. Beside the fireplace there sat a basket of dry chips that Emily had gathered and brought into the cabin the morning we left. On the table were a few scattered bread crumbs from the last breakfast we had eaten before we had left in such haste. On the floor was a pan with some scraps of dried molded meat where I had fed our dog.

As I gazed around, I saw the sash and glass had disappeared from our cabin window. The morning we left our home, Father had left a sack of cornmeal in the cabin and the Indians found mother's big wash kettle and had built a fire in the yard, boiled water and made mush from the cornmeal. There lay the big kettle tipped over, the fragments of the mush still adhering to its sides.

Mother was very tired and worn out from the long ride. Father brought in the strawticks and placed them on the bedsteads. He then carried in the feather beds and put them on top of the strawticks while we girls brought in the pillows and blankets and placed them on the beds so she could lie down and rest.

While Wash Smith drove the cattle into the lot and unhitched, unharnessed and fed the horses, Father and I washed the cupboard shelves and carried the dishes into the cabin and put them back into the cupboard. Emily scoured the pot bench and got it ready and we brought the kitchen utensils in and turned them upside down on the bench just as Mother always had kept them. We scrubbed the puncheon floor, carried in our clothes and hung them on their pegs.

Now everything was in its place just as it had been two years ago when we fled in such haste. Everything looked so natural I could hardly realize that we had been away at all.

Soon the Indians came in to welcome us back. I know they were really glad to have us come back. They had nothing against us in the first place but we had harbored Wash Smith when they thought he deserved to be tomahawked and scalped, so we had to go. When Wash Smith finished his work at the stable and came into the cabin, the Indians didn't say anything but an Indian never forgets or forgives and they didn't look at him very friendly.

Soon we saw Chief Wishecomaque coming up the hill toward our cabin. He was carrying our sash and glass in his arms. He came in the cabin and handed it to Father who took it. After thanking him, he placed it back into the window where it belonged. The Indians hadn't meant to steal it, they had only borrowed it to make a window in their chief's lodge and when the chief saw we had come back he returned it to us.

Rolling Thunder came along with the other Indians to welcome us home. Now he was twelve corn plantings old and had the same noiseless tread. He had the same bow and arrow. I wondered if in the two years that I had been away if he had let one single arrow fly or whether he was just taking aim at everything and kept his arrows like he used to do. He had the same little hatchet, but instead of the old broken bladed dagger, he now carried a real scalping knife in his belt and he had attached a bright glittering tomahawk to his outfit.

After the Indians went away and we had eaten our evening lunch and sister Emily and I had washed the dishes and placed them back on their shelves, we went outside and sat down on our hickory log door step. I can remember yet how clean that night air smelled, not like the crowded conditions at Keokuk where there were so many white people littering up the country and at night one could only hear the vile hooting laughter of the drunken men who were reveling at the bar across the way. Out here I could hear the voices of the little insects praising their creator with their songs in the night. I could hear the horses munching the grass where Wash Smith had staked them out to graze and the lowing of the tired cattle out there in the lot.

Beneath the low hanging branches of the trees, I could see the beautiful Iowa River shining and shimmering in the bright moonlight. There were hundreds of little fireflies flashing and vanishing like little flames of fire. I remembered how Rolling Thunder had once told me they were little candles that the witches were carrying while they were out searching for human souls to destroy.

A little owl hooted out from a tree above our heads. He was angry because we were there and the little feathered mite was telling us in no uncertain terms to get out and leave his dominion alone.

"Mary Ann, do you think he is the same little owl that was here in this tree above our cabin two years ago before we went away from our home to live in Keokuk?" Emily asked.

"Really, I don't know, Emily," I answered. "Anyway, he sure sounds like he was the same owl."

Just as I said this there came a fierce scream of a panther that came prowling down the trail that ran along back of our cabin and Mother called from inside the house, "Girls, it is time to come inside now and get ready for bed."

Figure 21: John Wolcott Adams, Artist. 1921. Library of Congress.
Image in the public domain.

18.

The Sheep, the Kitten, and the Hen

Emily and I had nearly all of the housework to do. Now I was ten years old and strong for my age. Emily was only seven, but she was a good girl to work and was willing to learn and tried hard to do as she was told. Father would help us with the work when he would be around the house. No matter what a failure we would make with our cooking, he would praise us in our efforts, which would encourage us to go on.

After our housework was finished, we were given time to play and we built a playhouse under the giant oak tree that stood like a sentinel beside our log cabin.

Our pet sheep insisted on staying there with us. He would mill around and stick his nose into everything we would try to do until we would get disgusted with his behavior and try to get rid of him. We couldn't get rid of him, though, for we couldn't drive him out, for he wouldn't be driven. Neither could we lead him, for he refused to be led, but we would both get behind him and push him out which didn't do any good either, for he would circle round and trot right back inside our playhouse again. He would act so cute about it, we then would feel sorry for him and let him stay. When we would go inside the cabin, he would lie down inside our play house and sleep until we would come out again and then he would get up to play.

One day after our work was finished and we came out to play, our pet sheep did not get up, nor did he ever get up again. A rattlesnake had bit him on the nose and he was too sick to get up. His eyes were swollen shut and his head was twice its natural size. There was nothing we could do for him and he suffered so intensely that we were glad when he could die and end his suffering. We all felt very bad about our pet sheep. He was almost like one of us and we grieved a long time after he was gone.

While we were living in Keokuk, the citizens would gather on various afternoons and hunt out the snakes and after killing them, place them in piles.

They put all the rattlesnakes in one pile, all the black snakes in another, while the spreading adders, garter snakes, hoop snakes and all the other kind of snakes were placed each in its own pile. When evening came on there would always be a larger pile of rattlesnakes than any other kind, for at that period of time they were more prevalent here in Iowa Territory than any other kind of snake.

This gave me an idea, and after a rattlesnake had killed our pet sheep, I meant to have revenge. Whenever I had time to do so, I hunted them instead of just killing the ones that were coiled in my path. Although I was only a child, I certainly did my part toward ridding the country of rattlesnakes. About the same time that we had to give up our pet sheep, Emily's kitten disappeared.

Mother couldn't eat all kinds of food like the rest of us. Father, sister Emily and I could eat cornbread, use brown or maple sugar or we could sweeten our food with honey that we gathered from the bee trees. We could drink coffee made from parched wheat or barley but Father always provided real coffee and white flour and white sand sugar for Mother. In these more modern days people call it granulated sugar but then it was called white sand sugar.

Nearly every day some Indians would come to our cabin and search around and if they chanced to see anything they wanted, they would ask Mother to give it to them. They would divide what they had with us and they thought we should do the same with them.

Father had made a large walnut chest for Mother which had a lock and key. She kept her groceries locked in it because groceries were very expensive and not even her own family could afford to eat of them, neither could she afford to divide with other people. When Mother saw the Indians coming, she would sit on her walnut chest and the Indian's manners were too good to ask her to unlock the chest so they could see inside it. This was how she was able to keep her groceries and also their good will.

One day we saw them coming and Mother hastened to the chest and both Emily and I climbed on it beside her. The Indians came in the cabin and there were so many of them they filled the cabin until almost all the standing room was taken. Emily's kitten was sitting in the window of the cabin basking in the sunlight. There was one squaw among them who had on a large loose blouse and we saw her gather up Emily's kitten and hide it under her loose blouse. Mother was afraid of the Indians and she told us to say nothing, for the kitten would come home when she would let loose of it, but it never came home. Emily never saw her kitten again.

I went down to the Indian camp several times and hunted for it and when I couldn't find it, I asked Rolling Thunder what the squaw had done with the kitten. He told me she cooked it and made soup for her family. Emily cried when she learned the squaw had cooked her kitten and I felt sorry for her because she thought so much of it. She had carried it in her arms all the way from Keokuk and now for such a gruesome thing to happen seemed too bad. Father told her she shouldn't have fed it so much then it would not have been so fat and perhaps would not have landed in the soup kettle.

Now, our pet sheep and Emily's kitten were gone, but mother still had her chickens. In the daytime we kept them in a little park that Father had built for them and at night we would put them in our log stable. One hen had set and hatched a dozen little fluffy balls that we called baby chicks. We always kept them in a box in the house at night. The Indians had never seen tame chickens so they took great interest in watching them. One brave in particular would come to our place several times every day to see them. Mother got tired of him hanging around our place so much and to get rid of him, she gave him the old rooster and told him to take it and go home, which he did. All the Indians took great delight in watching the rooster and would laugh loud when he would crow.

Then one day the same brave came back to our place and asked for a hen. Mother didn't want to give her hens away. She wanted to keep them to lay eggs to use in our cooking. She pretended she could not understand what he wanted, but he kept on trying to make her understand that he wanted her to give him a hen. At last, in desperation, he leaped up on a chair, and imitating a rooster, he flapped his arms as if they were wings, crowing, "Coo, coo, coo, oo, o." He then exclaimed in English, "Him wants squaw." We all had a good laugh at the show he put on, and Mother could not refuse him any longer and gave him a hen. He took her under his arm and walked proudly down the hill toward the camp.

The Indians did not cook and eat their chickens for they were too precious and rare a thing to eat, but they kept them to play with and cared for them even better than their own babies.

Figure 22: Girl with kitten

19

A Bygone Era

The immigrants were still coming down the rivers, through the woods, over the hills and through the valleys. Stopping at nothing and spreading deeper and wider until now in the year of 1842 they were advancing upon us. The silence of our great wilderness was broken. Men, women and children came on, lured by the tales they had been told about the rich, black soil and how easy it was to gain a home of their own in the new territory.

From the east and south they bore down upon us. All along the roads we could see them coming with their worn-out wagon covers flapping in the breeze and we could hear the screeching and groaning of their axle trees that were cussing the driver and crying aloud for grease.

The wagons were loaded with bedding, cooking utensils, churns, wash tubs and there were always a raft of children hanging on in various places upon the load and usually a plow tied on behind.

There were men who came from the east on horseback and wore store clothes and stovepipe hats. These were mostly land sharks, speculators, traders, preachers, lawyers, money-grabbers and always the crooks who were floating farther and farther west.

The human stream flowed on, until deep ruts were worn down by the wheels of the heavy wagons and even the grass between the ruts was trampled down by the feet of the weary oxen.

From every direction we could hear the ringing of the axes as they felled the ancient trees and at night the country would be lit up from the burning brush heaps that had been cleared from the ground through the day. They would cut and roll logs for a cabin and a small stable after which they would split rails for their fencing.

The cabins first constructed were something like a cross between and Indian hut and a hoop cabin. But after more settlers came in, they would get together and have a cabin raising. These later cabins were built of logs that were notched together at the corners. The top was ribbed with poles and then covered with clap boards they had split from trees. A puncheon floor was then laid down and a stick chimney run up.

They would cut a hole in the side of the cabin for a door, make a heavy door shutter and hang it on hinges. The door was fastened with old fashioned wooden latches. For a friend or neighbor or even for a traveler the latch string always hung out, for the pioneer of the Iowa Territory was hospitable and entertained visitors to the best of his ability.

A window was made in the cabin by cutting out a hole in the side or end about two feet square and covered with greased paper to admit the light and air. Quite often there was nothing whatever over the window and sometimes there was not even a hole cut for a window but the cracks between the logs where there was no clinking or daubing let in the light and fresh air.

A one-legged bedstead was made by cutting a stick in the proper length, then boring holes at one end that were one and a half inches in diameter at right angles, and the same size holes corresponding with those in the logs of the cabin. They inserted the poles in these holes, then upon the poles clapboards were laid or sometimes they took lined bark and interwove it consecutively from pole to pole. Upon this structure they laid their bed.

We had real bedsteads and other furniture too, for my father had been a cabinet-maker before we came to Iowa Territory. He had owned a cabinet shop in Green Castle, Indiana and he knew how to make first-class furniture. He made a nice walnut chest just like the one he had made for Mother, except a smaller one, and gave it to me the day I was 12 years old. He fashioned a little tray in one end for my handkerchiefs and ribbons and other small articles. It was a very nice chest and I have always valued it very highly.

We had no cook stoves in those days. The cooking was done in pots, pans, kettles and skillets on, above and around the big fireplace. The pioneer women were good cooks. They made excellent cornbread, much better than we ever know anything about in these modern days. I don't know why this was so - whether they knew more about stirring up the corn pone or whether it was better by baking in the old-fashioned oven over the coals in the fireplace instead of a cook stove like we have now.

If a house was to be raised, every man in the country would turn out and often the women turned out, too. While the men cut, piled and rolled logs, the women cooked dinner over a bonfire. If there happened to be a cabin near, they prepared the dinner there and carried it to the men. In the meanwhile, the young women would gather at some cabin in the neighborhood and quilt.

When night would come the young people would throw a party and dance on the puncheon floor of the new cabin. Sometimes the joists in the cabin were not high enough for a tall fellow to dance under them without striking his head against them. In that case the tall fellows would dance in the middle of the cabin and the shorter ones on either side.

In those far-off days the young people danced differently than they do now. They each selected a puncheon board and to the tune of a fiddle, they would shuffle from one end of the board to the other, then turn and shuffle back again, etc. Sometimes there would be an accident by one end of a puncheon tipping up and striking someone in the face but this did not often happen.

I never liked to hear a fiddle played in a church, for the sound of it always reminded me of the pioneer dances. Not very long ago I made that remark to one of our neighbors (John Hogson) who remembered those pioneer days too.

"Just call it a 'violin,' Mary Ann," he said. "Then it won't sound so bad." Nevertheless, a fiddle is a fiddle, and you can call it a violin or whatever you please, I still say a fiddle is out of its rightful place in a church.

In 1843 a man came to our neighborhood, built one of those log cabins and started to sell liquor, but the neighbors gathered and took the law in their own hands. After giving him a nice little coat, and also a pair of trousers made of tar and feathers, they told him to leave the country, which indeed he hastened to do.

In those pioneer days people didn't clique around in little bunches here and there like they do in these days. Then everyone was a friend to everyone else. At the public gatherings, everybody was treated just the same. If a neighbor fell sick and needed care and attention the whole neighborhood was interested and was always ready to do whatever they could for them. If a man killed a beef, deer or hog, everyone in the neighborhood was given a piece of it, which is a very good way for a neighborhood to get along together.

Some of the settlers new in the Iowa Territory did some very foolish things. One woman got up from her bed in the middle of the night and went out of doors with her feet bare, which was indeed a very foolish thing to do. As she stepped off the log doorstep, a rattlesnake bit her on the heel. She called to her husband and asked him to get up and help her but he didn't understand the snares that lurked in this wild country and didn't believe a snake had bitten her, so he refused to get up. He said afterwards that he just supposed she had hurt her heel on a splinter from the log. When there was nothing done for her, it wasn't long until the snake virus had entered her bloodstream and she only lived a few hours.

Some of the settlers who came to Iowa Territory in the year of 1842 were very superstitious. If you started to go someplace and forgot to take along something and had to go back to get it, you must sit down on a chair before starting out again or you would have bad luck.

If you had warts on your hands and wanted to get rid of them, just pick up a stick and put a notch in it for every wart on your hand then drop the stick in the road. Whoever picked up the stick would get the warts on their hands as they would leave your own.

If a dog howled out it was a sign there would soon be a death in the neighborhood but that could be prevented if you jerked off your shoe and placed the bottom of your shoe against the bottom of your foot, thus causing the dog to stop howling and consequently no death would occur.

It was a bad omen to hear an owl screech near a graveyard and if you had a ringing in your ear, it was a death knell and you would die within a year.

But we all got along well together. There was no hatred or malice or jealousy among us for we were all on the same level. Many a pioneer can remember the happiest time of his life as that time when he lived in one of those comfortable old log cabins in the neighborhood where he loved his neighbor as himself.

The End.

Epilogue

I hope you've found as much joy in reading Mary Ann's writings as I have. I believe that by keeping her words alive, we honor not only her, but also the hardships and sacrifices endured by those before us. Thank you for contributing to this endeavor.

It is not known why Mary Ann stopped her writing at age thirteen. Perhaps she saw this as the end of her childhood.

Mary Ann and husband Benjamin Mills remained in Richland, IA until 1855. Mary Ann's maternal grandfather, Richard Moore, died in Washington, IA on April 29, 1855. Benjamin and Mary Ann moved to Newton, Jasper County, IA soon after his death, where Benjamin purchased land. Mary Ann's father John Maulsby also moved to Jasper County along with his children Samuel, Avarilla and Martin. Richard's wife Rebecca remained in Washington and lived out the rest of her life there, living with son William and family.

About 1856, Benjamin, Mary Ann and children, as well as Mary Ann's father John moved to Hardin County, IA. Benjamin and Mary Ann settled in the Quaker community of New Providence. John made his home in Pleasant Township, just four miles away. By 1870, John moved to Lincoln, Putnam Co., MO and was living with his son Samuel and family. He died there in 1891.

Figure 23: Richard Moore, Rebecca (Embree) Moore

Genealogy

The following is correct to the best of my knowledge and research, but I must regretfully admit it is certain to contain errors.

Mary Ann Maulsby Mills

Mary Ann's Parents:

Father: John Cox Maulsby
Birth: 14 Apr 1803 in Indiana or Tennessee
Marriage: Sarah C "Sally" Moore, 09 Mar 1827 in Putnam, IN
Death: 08 Dec 1891 in Unionville, Putnam, MO
Burial: Unionville Cemetery, Unionville, MO
Father: William Maulsby (b) 25 Jan 1774 PA (d) 12 Feb 1806 TN
Mother: Mary Cox (b) 1781 IN (d) After 1806
Married: 17 Apr 1804 in Jefferson, TN

Mother: Sarah C "Sally" Moore
Birth: 1805 in Ohio
Death: 18 May 1849 in Keokuk County, IA
Burial: unknown, but likely in the Friends Cemetery, Richland, IA
Father: Richard Jenkins Moore Jr. (b) 7 Sep 1786 GA (d) 29 Apr 1855 Washington County, IA (bur) Moore Cemetery, Washington, IA
Mother: Rebecca Embree (b) 2 Dec 1789 GA (d) 23 Dec 1870 Washington County, IA (bur) Moore Cemetery, Washington, IA

Mary Ann's Siblings:

Emily Maria Maulsby
Birth: 16 Jul 1834 in Indiana
Marriage: John Ward Benson, 16 Aug 1854 in Washington, IA
Children: Ignacius, Henry, Samuel, Orphelia, Jenetta, Joseph, Franklin, Mary
Death: 14 Apr 1913 in Hardin County, IA
Burial: Sheppard Cemetery, Gifford, Hardin County, IA

John Maulsby
Birth: 1837 in Washington Co., IA.
Death: Oct 1837 in IA
Burial: Section 29, Washington County, IA on private property. A stone marker was placed in 2009 by Marla Rhodes and Deanna Overman, Mary Ann's 2nd great granddaughters, and Karlene Kingery. It is near where it is believed Mary Ann's wilderness cabin once stood. The stone is engraved with his name, October 1837, and "His spirit will always be with us."

Samuel A. Maulsby
Birth: 01 May 1837 in Washington Co., IA
Marriage: Eliza Alice Stine
Children: Minnie, Jeff, Florence, Walter, Thomas, Icy, Grover
Death: 11 Feb 1886 in Unionville, Putnam, MO
Burial: Unionville Cemetery, Putnam County, MO

Avarilla Emma Maulsby
Birth: 19 Jul 1840 in IA
Marriage: Rufus Lewis St. John
Children: Sarah, Ruben, John, Samuel, William, Mae, Philina
Death: 12 Feb 1888 in Howland, MO
Burial: Mendota Cemetery, Putnam County, MO

Martin Van Buren Maulsby
Birth: 11 Jul 1844 in Washington, IA
Marriage: Ann Eliza Kearns, 1878
Children: Lena, Fred, Frank, Mary, Abby
Death: 24 Jan 1919 in Eldora, Hardin, IA
Burial: Eldora City Cemetery, Hardin County, IA

Husband Benjamin Mills

Birth: 12 Feb 1829 in Lost Creek, Jefferson, TN
Marriage: 15 Oct 1849 in Keokuk, Richland, IA
Death: 21 Nov 1897 in Hardin County, IA
Burial: Honey Creek Cemetery, New Providence, Hardin County, IA
Father: John Mills (b) 25 Aug 1807 TN (d) 10 Nov 1853 Iowa (bur) Richland, IA
Mother: Mary "Polly" Janeway (b) 1810 TN (d) 28 Jul 1846 Richland, Keokuk, IA (bur) unknown

Benjamin and Mary Ann's Children:

Charles D Mills
Birth: 14 Feb 1851 in Richland, Adair, IA
Marriage 1: Alice R Bull, 29 May 1877 in Hardin County, IA
Children: Otis, Viola, Lemuel, Olive, Oliver
Marriage 2: Amanda Gregory, 1 April 1926 in Dallas Co., MO
Death: 25 Jun 1935 in Burwell, Garfield, NE
Burial: Cottonwood Cemetery, Burwell, Garfield County, NE

Ira Thaddeus Mills

Birth: 24 Feb 1853 in Richland, Adair, IA
Marriage: Jane L. Presnell, 15 Jun 1884 in Cherokee, IA
Children: Clinton Louis, Nelie Lois
Death: 13 Apr 1938 in Clemons, Marshall, IA
Burial: Honey Creek Cemetery, New Providence, Hardin County, IA

Sarah Jane Mills

Birth: 22 Mar 1856 in Jasper, IA
Death: 12 Jun 1876 in New Providence, Hardin County, IA
Burial: Honey Creek Cemetery, New Providence, Hardin County, IA

John William Mills

Birth: 17 Nov 1858 in Providence, Hardin, IA
Marriage: Adelia Jane Upford
Children: Sarah Lodemia
Death: 28 Nov 1949 in Farnhamville, Calhoun, IA
Burial: Cedar Cemetery, Rinard, Calhoun County, IA

Mary Louise Mills

Birth: 07 Feb 1862 in New Providence, Hardin, IA
Marriage: Silas Stinson, 08 Dec 1886 in Hardin, IA
Children: Eathyl Muriel
Death: 02 Jul 1963 in Iowa City, Johnson, IA
Burial: Honey Creek Cemetery, New Providence, IA

Henry Maulsby Mills

Birth: 27 Oct 1864 in Hardin County, IA
Marriage: Mary Edith Peck, 19 Feb 1896 in Rolfe, Pocahontas, IA
Children: George Ray
Death: 22 Feb 1932 in Watertown, Codington, SD
Burial: Mount Hope Cemetery, Watertown, Codington County, SD

Macy J. Mills

Birth: 03 May 1867 in Providence, Hardin, IA
Marriage: Minnie Mann, 13 Mar 1892 in Hardin, IA
Children: Veva C.
Death: 01 Dec 1928 in Altamont, Labette, KS
Burial: Mount Pleasant Cemetery, Altamont, Labette County, KS

Louis Benjamin Mills

Birth: 13 Nov 1869 in Providence Twp, Hardin, IA
Marriage: Carrie S. McFarland, 20 Mar 1894 in Hardin, IA
Children: Merle, Millard Ulysses Kinsey, Jessie
Death: 31 Aug 1946 in New Providence, IA
Burial: Honey Creek Cemetery, New Providence, Hardin County, IA

Ava Rilla Mills

Birth: 13 Feb 1873 in Providence, Hardin, IA
Marriage: George Washington Bailey
Children: Bessie Agnes, George, Warren H., Beulah, Ruth
Death: 10 Nov 1964 in Iowa Falls, Hardin, IA
Burial: Hubbard Cemetery, Hubbard, Hardin County, IA

Martha Lodemia Mills

Birth: 31 Dec 1876 in Providence, Hardin, IA
Marriage: James Everett Huffman, 15 Jun 1910 in Hardin, IA
Children: Merton Everette
Death: 17 Jul 1954 in Des Moines, Polk County, IA
Burial: Lancaster Cemetery, Lancaster, Los Angeles County, California

Pedigrees

Relationship: Mary Ann Maulsby to Benjamin Mills

Benjamin Mills is the 2nd cousin of Mary Ann Maulsby

Great grandparent

John Maulsby Sr
b: 1735
Limerick, PA, USA
d: 08 Mar 1809
Lost Creek, TN, USA

Lydia John
b: 07 Sep 1745
Nantmel, Chester, Pennsylvania, USA
d: 1816
Lost Creek, Jefferson, Tennessee, USA

Paternal grandfather

William Maulsby
b: 25 Jan 1774
York County, Pennsylvania, USA
d: 12 Apr 1806
Tennessee, USA

Great-aunt

Sarah (Sallie) Maulsby
b: 20 Dec 1776
York, Pennsylvania, USA
d: 28 Nov 1842
Lost Creek, Jefferson, Tennessee, USA

Father

John Cox Maulsby
b: 14 Apr 1803
IN or TN
d: 08 Dec 1891
Unionville, Putnam, Missouri, USA

1st cousin 1x removed

John Mills
b: 25 Aug 1807
New Market, Jefferson, Tennessee, USA
d: 10 Nov 1853
Jefferson County, Iowa, USA

Self

Mary Ann Maulsby
b: 06 Jun 1830
Green Castle, Putnam County, Indiana, USA
d: 17 Jul 1909
New Providence, Hardin, Iowa, USA

2nd cousin

Benjamin Mills
b: 12 Feb 1829
Lost Creek, Jefferson, Tennessee, USA
d: 21 Nov 1897
Hardin County, Iowa, USA

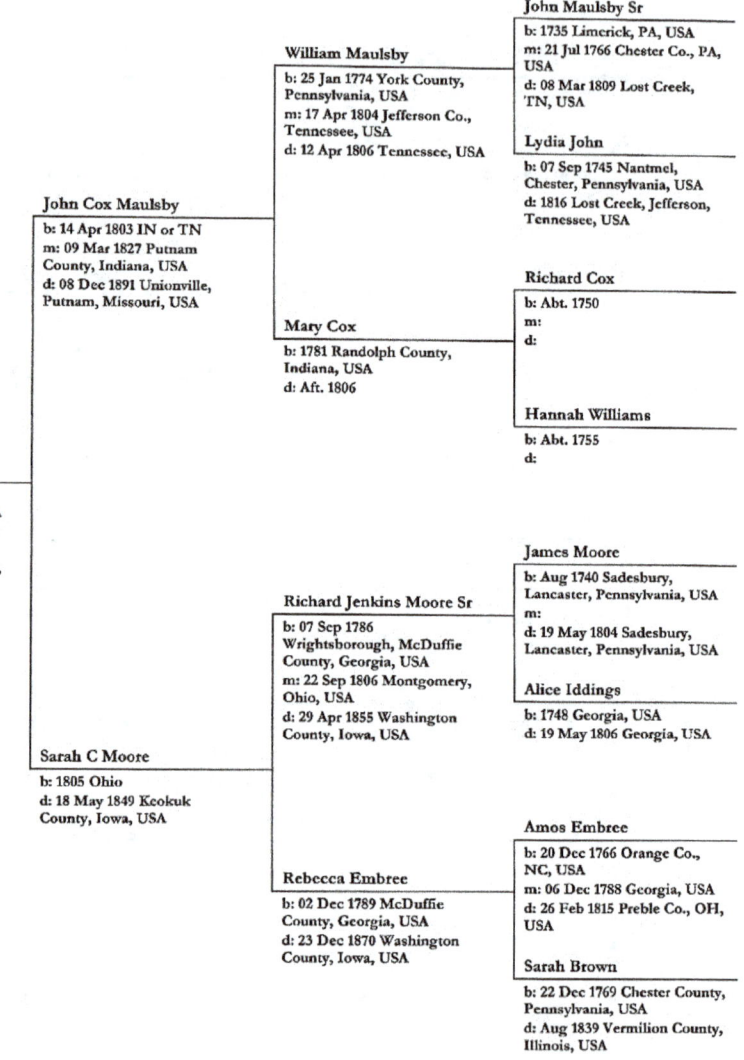

John Maulsby Sr

b: 1735 Limerick, PA, USA
m: 21 Jul 1766 Chester Co., PA, USA
d: 08 Mar 1809 Lost Creek, TN, USA

William Maulsby

b: 25 Jan 1774 York County, Pennsylvania, USA
m: 17 Apr 1804 Jefferson Co., Tennessee, USA
d: 12 Apr 1806 Tennessee, USA

Lydia John

b: 07 Sep 1745 Nantmel, Chester, Pennsylvania, USA
d: 1816 Lost Creek, Jefferson, Tennessee, USA

John Cox Maulsby

b: 14 Apr 1803 IN or TN
m: 09 Mar 1827 Putnam County, Indiana, USA
d: 08 Dec 1891 Unionville, Putnam, Missouri, USA

Richard Cox

b: Abt. 1750
m:
d:

Mary Cox

b: 1781 Randolph County, Indiana, USA
d: Aft. 1806

Hannah Williams

b: Abt. 1755
d:

Mary Ann Maulsby

b: 06 Jun 1830 Green Castle, Putnam County, Indiana, USA
m: 15 Oct 1849 Keokuk, Iowa, USA
d: 17 Jul 1909 New Providence, Hardin, Iowa, USA

James Moore

b: Aug 1740 Sadesbury, Lancaster, Pennsylvania, USA
m:
d: 19 May 1804 Sadesbury, Lancaster, Pennsylvania, USA

Richard Jenkins Moore Sr

b: 07 Sep 1786 Wrightsborough, McDuffie County, Georgia, USA
m: 22 Sep 1806 Montgomery, Ohio, USA
d: 29 Apr 1855 Washington County, Iowa, USA

Alice Iddings

b: 1748 Georgia, USA
d: 19 May 1806 Georgia, USA

Sarah C Moore

b: 1805 Ohio
d: 18 May 1849 Keokuk County, Iowa, USA

Amos Embree

b: 20 Dec 1766 Orange Co., NC, USA
m: 06 Dec 1788 Georgia, USA
d: 26 Feb 1815 Preble Co., OH, USA

Rebecca Embree

b: 02 Dec 1789 McDuffie County, Georgia, USA
d: 23 Dec 1870 Washington County, Iowa, USA

Sarah Brown

b: 22 Dec 1769 Chester County, Pennsylvania, USA
d: Aug 1839 Vermilion County, Illinois, USA

Benjamin Mills
b: 12 Feb 1829 Lost Creek, Jefferson, Tennessee, USA
m: 15 Oct 1849 Keokuk, Iowa, USA
d: 21 Nov 1897 Hardin County, Iowa, USA

John Mills
b: 25 Aug 1807 New Market, Jefferson, Tennessee, USA
m: 1827 Jefferson Co., Tennessee, USA
d: 10 Nov 1853 Jefferson County, Iowa, USA

Mary "Polly" Janeway
b: 1810 Strawberry Plains, Jefferson, TN
d: 28 Jul 1846 Richland, Keokuk, Iowa, USA

William Mills Sr
b: 19 Jan 1770 Guilford Co., North Carolina, USA
m: 22 Oct 1799 Lost Creek, Jefferson, Tennessee, USA
d: 08 Aug 1862 Jasper Co., Iowa, USA

Sarah (Sallie) Maulsby
b: 20 Dec 1776 York, Pennsylvania, USA
d: 28 Nov 1842 Lost Creek, Jefferson, Tennessee, USA

Benjamin Janeway
b: 1789 North Carolina, USA
m: 1807 TN
d: Mar 1862 Strawberry Plains, Jefferson, Tennessee, USA

Mary Jane Childers
b: 1790 Lost Creek, Jefferson, Tennessee, USA
d: 1825 Lost Creek, Jefferson, Tennessee, USA

John Mills
b:
m: Guilford County, North Carolina, USA; Married at New Garden Monthly Meeting.
d:

Sarah Williams
b:
d:

John Maulsby Sr
b: 1735 Limerick, PA, USA
m: 21 Jul 1766 Chester Co., PA, USA
d: 08 Mar 1809 Lost Creek, TN, USA

Lydia John
b: 07 Sep 1745 Nantmel, Chester, Pennsylvania, USA
d: 1816 Lost Creek, Jefferson, Tennessee, USA

Joseph Janeway
b: 1761 North Carolina, USA
m:
d: 1830 Strawberry Plains, Jefferson, Tennessee, USA

Susan Medearis
b: 1760 North Carolina, USA
d: 1830 Strawberry Plains, Jefferson, Tennessee, USA

John Robert Childress Jr
b: 02 Dec 1759 Albemarle County, Virginia, USA
m: 1779 VA
d: 11 Jan 1849 Bull Run Valley, Knox, Tennessee, USA

Elizabeth Lindsay
b: 1750 VA
d:

Acknowledgements

I would like to express my most sincere gratitude to Karlene Kingery for the meticulous and detailed work she did in editing Mary Ann's writings in her book, "A True Pioneer Story; Memories of a Pioneer Girl." I strongly suggest anyone interested in Mary Ann's story and life read her book as well. Unfortunately, it is now out of print but can be found in many libraries in Iowa. She, along with two of Mary Ann's great-great granddaughters, put a great deal of time and effort into locating the likely location of Mary Ann's cabin in the woods and specifically, little John's burial site. A marker stone sits there today because of their efforts.

I want to extend my deepest gratitude to my brother, Travis Biggs, for his exceptional talent in designing the cover. His expertise is truly remarkable.

Thank you as well to my dear husband, who has never quite understood my fascination with all things pioneer, but graciously tolerated my countless hours of obsessive research behind computer screens. You're a keeper, honey.

I must grant my deepest and most heartfelt appreciation and adoration to my dear mother. Although she is no longer in this world with me, she lives forever in my heart and in every word I type. She gave me the gift of a love for genealogy. It is an interest that has stayed with me for decades and I likely would have never had if she had not sparked it.

Thank you, Dad for encouraging and supporting me. You never understood my fascination with genealogy and pioneers, but you didn't need to. From walking cemeteries with me to rescuing me from one, you were always there for me.

Last but not least! – my dear son. You offered to be the first to buy this book even though it is about the last thing you'd be interested in. You are a truly sweet soul and the best thing I've ever had or done in my life. I love you with all that I am.

www.ingramcontent.com/pod-product-compliance
Lightning Source LLC
Chambersburg PA
CBHW060326130626
46553CB00003B/928